PURPOSE DRIVEN RETIREMENT

(AND MISSION)

A Biblical Guide to Faith, Stewardship, and Living With Purpose in the Next Chapter of Life

Stuart Hunsicker

Founder, Purpose Driven Retirement Planners

Purpose Driven Press

Copyright

Published by Purpose Driven Press.

ISBN: 979-8-9977452-0-2

Published August 2026

Disclaimer

This book is intended for general educational and informational purposes only. It is not individualized investment, financial, tax, legal, accounting, insurance, Social Security, Medicare, retirement-plan, theological, pastoral, or other professional advice. Laws, regulations, tax rules, government benefits, plan provisions, insurance contracts, and financial-market conditions can change, and their application depends on individual circumstances.

Examples are illustrative. Before implementing a strategy, consult the appropriate qualified professionals and verify current rules with authoritative sources. References to Scripture are used to illuminate principles of stewardship, responsibility, generosity, service, contentment, family, and purpose. Readers are encouraged to study the cited passages in context and in their preferred Bible translation.

Unless a Bible translation is specifically identified, Scripture references in the narrative are summaries or paraphrases intended to point the reader back to the cited passage rather than reproduce a particular translation verbatim.

Nothing in this book creates an advisory, fiduciary, attorney-client, accountant-client, insurance, pastoral, or other professional relationship.

Dedication

To my family, for being my greatest source of purpose.

To my faith, for keeping me grounded in what truly matters.

To my team, for believing in the work we do and the people we serve.

And to the clients I have had the privilege of working with over the years. Your lives, questions, challenges, successes, and experiences have shaped me as an advisor and helped create the perspective I now bring to every family I serve.

This book is, in many ways, the product of all of you.

How to Use This Book

This book is designed to be used, not simply read.

Retirement planning is still the principal subject of these pages. Faith is the foundation beneath it: a way to think about stewardship, responsibility, family, generosity, contentment, service, and the purpose of the years ahead.

As you read, keep returning to four questions:

What matters most?

What does my money need to do?

What is enough?

Does this decision help me live the retirement—and mission—I said I wanted?

Write in the margins. Complete the exercises. Revisit the chapters as life changes. This is not meant to be a book you finish once and forget. It is meant to be a book you return to and use.

Contents

Introduction

Retirement Is Not the End of Your Mission

Most retirement books begin with money. This one begins with purpose.

Money matters. It determines choices, creates security, funds experiences, protects independence, and can become an extraordinary tool for generosity. But money is not the destination. It is a resource entrusted to us for a season.

A biblical view of retirement does not require us to reject enjoyment, travel, comfort, or the bucket list. It asks us to hold those things in balance with stewardship, family, giving, service, gratitude, and the possibility that some of our most meaningful work may happen after the career ends.

The question is not merely, "Can I afford to retire?" It is also, "What is this next chapter for?"

Throughout this book we will keep the same practical retirement principles: build the paycheck, manage investment risk, coordinate Social Security and pensions, plan taxes, prepare for healthcare and long-term care, protect family, and organize the estate. But we will also ask what Scripture can teach us about enough, responsibility, generosity, service, and legacy.

That balance matters. Faith should never be used as a sales technique, and a Bible verse should never substitute for sound financial analysis. The technical planning must remain technically sound. Faith provides the foundation for why we plan and how we decide what the plan is ultimately meant to accomplish.

Retirement can be a season of freedom. Freedom to enjoy. Freedom to serve. Freedom to give. Freedom to be present. Freedom to use the experience, relationships, resources, and time accumulated over a lifetime in ways that matter.

That is the retirement—and mission—we are going to plan for.

> **A Foundation of Stewardship**
> *The biblical idea of stewardship begins with the recognition that what we possess is not the whole measure of who we are. Resources carry responsibility. Planning is one way of caring well for what has been entrusted to us.*
> ***Scripture anchor: Matthew 25:14–30; 1 Corinthians 4:2***

Part I — Designing the Retirement You Actually Want

◆

Chapter 1

Retirement Isn't a Number

> **Purpose Before the Number**
> *Jesus repeatedly redirects attention from possessions toward the condition and direction of a life. A retirement number is useful only because of what it makes possible.*
> ***Scripture anchor: Luke 12:15***

Ask someone what they need in order to retire, and there's a good chance you'll hear a number.

"A million dollars."

"Two million."

"Ten thousand dollars a month."

"Enough to replace 80% of my income."

We've been conditioned to think about retirement this way.

Financial articles tell us how much we should have saved by a certain age. Online calculators ask us to enter our income, savings, and expected retirement date. Investment statements show us whether our account balances are growing.

Eventually, it becomes easy to believe that retirement is a mathematical equation:

Reach the number = retire successfully.

But I've met people with significant wealth who were terrified to retire.

I've also met people with far less money who were completely comfortable.

The difference wasn't always how much they had.

Often, it was how clearly they understood what their money needed to do.

That's why one of the biggest mistakes we can make when planning for retirement is starting with the number.

We need to start with the life.

What Does Retirement Actually Mean to You?

Think about the word *retirement* for a moment.

What picture comes to mind?

Maybe it's sitting on a beach.

Maybe it's playing golf on a Tuesday morning.

Maybe it's traveling across the country in an RV.

Maybe it's finally having time to work in the garden, go fishing, or restore the old car that's been sitting in the garage.

For some people, retirement doesn't mean stopping work at all.

It might mean leaving a demanding career and consulting two days a week.

It could mean starting the business you've always wanted to build.

It might mean teaching.

Volunteering.

Working at a golf course simply because you enjoy being there.

Or helping take care of grandchildren.

That's why asking, **"When do you want to retire?"** isn't enough.

A better question is:

"What are you retiring to?"

That's a much more interesting conversation.

If you've spent thirty or forty years building a career, your job probably provides more than a paycheck.

It provides structure.

Relationships.

Responsibility.

A sense of accomplishment.

Maybe even part of your identity.

Then one day, all of that changes.

Friday you're an executive, engineer, teacher, firefighter, business owner, federal employee, or manager.

Monday you're...retired.

That transition can be wonderful.

It can also be disorienting.

Financial independence gives you the ability to retire.

Purpose gives you a reason to enjoy it.

The Saturday Problem

Here's an exercise I sometimes use when talking about retirement.

Imagine your favorite Saturday.

You wake up without an alarm.

Maybe you have coffee on the porch.

You go to breakfast with your spouse.

You play golf, work around the house, see the grandchildren, go boating, take a drive, meet friends for dinner, or simply enjoy not having anywhere you have to be.

Sounds pretty good.

Now imagine doing it again Sunday.

Still good.

Monday?

Great.

Tuesday?

Absolutely.

Now do it for six months.

Then five years.

Then twenty years.

The point isn't that retirement has to become boring.

The point is that **retirement needs more than the absence of work.**

You need something you're moving toward.

That might be family.

Travel.

Faith.

Community.

Learning.

Adventure.

Service.

Health.

Relationships.

Creativity.

Or even another form of work.

Retirement gives you something extraordinarily valuable:

time.

The real question is what you're going to do with it.

The Three Stages of Retirement

Retirement often changes as we age.

The retirement you experience at 62 probably won't look exactly like the retirement you experience at 82.

For planning purposes, it can be helpful to think about retirement in three broad stages.

The Active Years

These are often the years people imagine when they picture retirement.

You're newly retired.

You're hopefully healthy.

You have energy.

And suddenly you have time.

These can be the years of travel, hobbies, golf, cruises, second homes, grandchildren, restaurants, and experiences.

Interestingly, these may also be some of the **most expensive years of retirement**.

That's something traditional retirement projections don't always communicate very well.

We sometimes assume spending will simply rise with inflation every year.

Real life may look very different.

A couple might spend considerably more at 65 than they do at 80 because they're actually doing more.

They're traveling.

They're eating out.

They're buying things.

They're helping family.

They're enjoying the freedom they spent decades working toward.

And that's okay.

The purpose of retirement planning isn't necessarily to minimize spending.

It's to make spending **sustainable**.

The Slower Years

At some point, retirement often begins to change.

Maybe the ten-hour flight to Europe doesn't sound quite as appealing anymore.

Maybe maintaining two homes becomes more trouble than it's worth.

Maybe golf goes from four days a week to two.

Life can become a little quieter.

Spending may shift as well.

Travel and entertainment expenses might decrease, while healthcare and convenience expenses begin increasing.

Your priorities may become more centered around family, comfort, and simplicity.

The Support Years

Later in retirement, independence itself can become one of the most important financial goals.

You may need help.

That doesn't necessarily mean nursing-home care.

It could mean someone helping around the house.

Transportation.

Meal preparation.

Home modifications.

Assisted living.

Home healthcare.

Or simply moving closer to family.

These years introduce an entirely different set of financial questions.

Where do you want to live?

Who would help you?

Would you want to remain in your home?

Could your home accommodate you physically?

What happens if one spouse needs care and the other doesn't?

How would you pay for it?

These aren't always enjoyable questions.

But answering them while you still have plenty of choices is much better than forcing your family to make those decisions during a crisis.

Your Retirement Number Depends on Your Retirement

Let's look at two hypothetical couples.

Meet Tom and Susan.

They retire at 65.

Their mortgage is paid off. They enjoy being home. They take one nice vacation each year, spend time with their grandchildren, and live relatively modestly.

They determine that they can comfortably live on $7,000 per month.

Now meet David and Karen.

They're also 65.

They want to travel internationally twice a year. They belong to a country club. They own a vacation property. They want to give money to their children and grandchildren while they're alive.

Their desired lifestyle requires $14,000 per month.

Who needs more money for retirement?

Obviously, David and Karen.

But here's the more important question:

Who has the better retirement?

There is no answer.

If Tom and Susan are living exactly the life they want, their retirement is successful.

If David and Karen are doing the same, theirs is successful too.

That's why comparing your retirement savings to your neighbor's—or to some number in an article—isn't particularly useful.

Their money has a different job.

Stop Asking, "Do I Have Enough?"

There's nothing wrong with asking whether you have enough money to retire.

Eventually, we absolutely need to answer that question.

But we first need to finish the sentence.

Enough money **for what?**

Enough to pay the bills?

Enough to travel?

Enough to maintain your home?

Enough to help your children?

Enough to survive a major market decline?

Enough if one spouse lives to 100?

Enough for healthcare?

Enough to leave an inheritance?

Those are different questions.

And they can produce very different answers.

This is where good retirement planning begins to separate itself from simple investment planning.

Investment planning asks:

"How should we invest the money?"

Retirement planning asks:

"What does the money need to accomplish?"

Only after we understand the second question can we intelligently answer the first.

The Retirement Paycheck

One of the biggest psychological changes in retirement is something that sounds very simple:

The paycheck stops.

For decades, money arrives on a predictable schedule.

Every two weeks.

Twice a month.

Once a month.

You know what is coming in.

You pay your bills.

You save some.

You spend some.

Then retirement arrives, and suddenly you may have several different sources of money.

Social Security.

A pension.

A 401(k).

An IRA.

Roth accounts.

Brokerage accounts.

Savings.

Annuities.

Rental income.

Maybe part-time work.

The question becomes:

How do all of these pieces work together to create the paycheck I need?

That is one of the central challenges of retirement.

Accumulation is largely about building assets.

Retirement is about converting those assets into **income, flexibility, security, and experiences**.

And that requires more planning than simply choosing a withdrawal percentage.

The Freedom Number

Instead of thinking about one giant retirement number, I prefer thinking about what we might call your **Freedom Number**.

Your Freedom Number is the amount of dependable income you need each month to support the life you want.

Start with the basics.

Housing.

Food.

Utilities.

Transportation.

Insurance.

Healthcare.

Taxes.

Then add the things that make retirement enjoyable.

Travel.

Dining out.

Golf.

Hobbies.

Entertainment.

Gifts.

Grandchildren.

Charitable giving.

Then consider the expenses that don't happen every month.

A new vehicle.

A roof.

A major vacation.

Home improvements.

Weddings.

Helping children.

Replacing appliances.

Those expenses are real even though they don't fit neatly into a monthly budget.

Now we have something useful.

Instead of saying:

"I think I need $2 million to retire."

You might say:

"We want $9,000 per month after taxes, plus $15,000 per year for travel, and we'd like to replace our vehicles every eight years."

Now we can plan.

We can determine how much Social Security might cover.

How much a pension might provide.

How much your investments need to generate.

How taxes affect those withdrawals.

And how much flexibility we need for the unexpected.

Your retirement has started becoming real.

What Matters Most?

> **Planning From the Inside Out**
> *A biblical retirement plan begins with priorities before products. Jesus teaches that where our treasure goes, our heart tends to follow. The practical planning question is therefore not only how much we have, but what our use of money says matters most.*
> ***Scripture anchor: Matthew 6:19-21***

Now we're going to return to the question from the introduction.

What matters most to you?

Take some time with this.

Not what you think you're supposed to say.

Not what sounds responsible.

What actually matters?

Imagine you're ten years into retirement and things have gone extremely well.

What happened?

Where are you living?

Who are you spending time with?

What are you doing?

What have you experienced?

Who have you helped?

What aren't you worried about anymore?

Those answers become the foundation of your plan.

Your Purpose Driven Action Step

Before moving to the next chapter, take out a piece of paper.

Better yet, sit down with your spouse or partner and answer these questions separately before comparing answers.

1. If money were not an issue, what would our ideal retirement look like?

Don't start by limiting yourself.

Dream first.

We'll deal with reality later.

2. What are the five things we most want to experience during the first ten years of retirement?

Be specific.

Not "travel."

Where?

Not "spend time with family."

Doing what?

3. Where do we want to live?

Current home?

Downsize?

Move closer to family?

Own two homes?

Move somewhere warmer?

4. Who do we want to help financially?

Children?

Grandchildren?

Parents?

Church?

Charities?

5. What would we regret not doing while we're healthy enough to do it?

This may be the most important question on the page.

6. What are we most afraid could go wrong financially?

Running out of money?

Market losses?

Taxes?

Healthcare?

Long-term care?

Losing a spouse?

Inflation?

Helping children too much?

7. What does "financial independence" mean to us?

Not to your neighbor.

Not to an article.

To you.

Write the answers down.

Because eventually every major financial decision in your retirement plan should connect back to something on this page.

The Goal Is Not to Die With the Most Money

> **The Rich Fool and the Danger of an Unused Life**
> *Luke 12 tells of a man who kept building larger barns for his abundance but never reached the life he assumed would come later. The warning is not against saving. It is against allowing accumulation to become the destination. Retirement assets should eventually serve life, family, generosity, and purpose.*
> ***Scripture anchor: Luke 12:16-21***

There's an uncomfortable idea worth discussing.

Some people become so focused on protecting their money that they forget why they accumulated it.

They worked for decades.

They saved diligently.

They invested.

They sacrificed.

Then retirement arrives—and they're afraid to spend anything.

Every vacation feels irresponsible.

Every large purchase creates anxiety.

The account balance becomes something that must constantly be protected.

Certainly, we don't want to spend recklessly.

Longevity matters.

Healthcare matters.

Inflation matters.

Unexpected expenses matter.

But there is another risk that rarely appears in financial-planning software.

The risk of reaching the end of your life with plenty of money but a long list of things you wish you had done.

You can leave money behind.

You can't leave unused time behind and come back for it later.

That doesn't mean spend everything.

It means your money should have a purpose.

Some of it may be intended to provide security.

Some may create income.

Some may be there for emergencies.

Some may be intended for your children.

Some may go to charity.

And some of it should probably be used to enjoy the life you spent decades working to create.

That's what makes retirement planning personal.

Your Money Needs a Job

> **Stewardship Gives Money an Assignment**
> *Stewardship is active. Resources are entrusted, managed, protected, and ultimately used. Giving every account a job turns wealth from an abstract score into a tool for provision, resilience, generosity, and mission.*
> ***Scripture anchor: Matthew 25:14-30***

By the end of this book, I want you to be able to look at your financial life differently.

Instead of seeing:

401(k): $800,000
IRA: $450,000
Savings: $100,000
Investment account: $300,000

I want you to see what those dollars are supposed to **do**.

Some dollars may create your retirement paycheck.

Some may protect the next five years of spending.

Some may be positioned for long-term growth.

Some may be reserved for healthcare.

Some may eventually go to your children.

Some may be intended for experiences.

Every dollar doesn't necessarily need the same job.

And if different dollars have different jobs, they may not all belong in the same investments or even the same types of accounts.

That's where retirement planning begins getting interesting.

But before we decide where the money should go, we need to understand something else.

We need to know **where you are today**.

Because there is always a distance between the retirement you want and the resources you currently have.

Sometimes that distance is surprisingly small.

Sometimes it's larger than expected.

Either way, our next job isn't to worry about it.

Our job is to measure it.

Because once we can measure the gap, we can begin building a strategy to close it.

And that's where planning really begins.

Chapter 2

Where Are You Today?

> **Count What Has Been Entrusted**
> *An honest inventory is not about pride or shame. It is an act of stewardship: understanding the resources, obligations, and responsibilities already in your care.*
> ***Scripture anchor: Luke 14:28***

Imagine you're planning a road trip.

You know exactly where you want to go. You've picked the destination, decided what you want to see along the way, and maybe even figured out when you'd like to arrive.

Then you open the map.

There's one piece of information you absolutely need before you can determine the route:

Where are you starting from?

Retirement planning works the same way.

In the last chapter, we talked about defining the retirement you actually want. We identified what matters most, what you'd like your life to look like, and what your money ultimately needs to accomplish.

That's the destination.

Now we need to find the little dot on the map that says:

YOU ARE HERE.

This is where retirement planning becomes more concrete.

And for some people, a little uncomfortable.

Because we're going to take an honest look at where you are financially today.

Not where you think you should be.

Not where your neighbor is.

Not where some financial article says someone your age ought to be.

Where **you** are.

Because we can't build a useful plan until we understand our starting point.

Financial Organization Is Financial Planning

> **Order Creates Capacity**
> *Good stewardship is difficult when no one knows what exists, where it is held, who owns it, or what happens next. Organization may not feel spiritual, but clarity can be an act of care for a spouse and family.*
> ***Scripture anchor: 1 Corinthians 14:40***

Over the years, I've noticed something interesting.

Many people don't have a financial planning problem.

They have a financial **organization** problem.

They've accumulated accounts throughout their lives.

A 401(k) from their current employer.

An old 401(k) from a company they left fifteen years ago.

An IRA.

A Roth IRA.

A savings account.

A brokerage account.

A pension.

Social Security.

Life insurance.

Maybe an annuity.

Maybe some company stock.

Maybe an old account they aren't even sure what to do with.

None of this happened because they were irresponsible.

Quite the opposite.

These accounts often exist because they were doing exactly what they were supposed to do at different stages of their lives.

The problem is that nobody ever stepped back and asked:

"How do all of these pieces work together?"

That's what we're going to do.

Before we start changing anything, we're going to organize it.

Build Your Retirement Balance Sheet

Businesses use balance sheets to understand their financial position.

You should too.

Fortunately, yours doesn't need to be complicated.

Take out a piece of paper and divide it into two columns.

On the left side write:

What We Own

On the right side write:

What We Owe

Let's start with what you own.

Retirement Accounts

List every retirement account you have.

That might include:

401(k)s

403(b)s

457 plans

Traditional IRAs

Roth IRAs

TSP accounts

SEP IRAs

SIMPLE IRAs

Cash balance plans

Other employer retirement plans

Write down the approximate value of each.

Don't worry about being exact to the penny.

We're trying to see the big picture.

Investment Accounts

Next, list investments outside retirement accounts.

Brokerage accounts.

Stocks.

Bonds.

Mutual funds.

ETFs.

Certificates of deposit.

Treasury securities.

Anything intended to help fund your future.

Cash

Now list your cash reserves.

Checking.

Savings.

Money market accounts.

Emergency funds.

Cash may not seem very exciting compared with investments, but in retirement it can become extremely important.

We'll talk later about why.

Real Estate

List your primary home and any other real estate you own.

Rental properties.

Vacation homes.

Land.

Commercial property.

Estimate the current market value and write down any debt associated with each property.

Other Assets

Depending on your situation, you might also have:

Business interests.

Stock options.

Deferred compensation.

Annuities.

Cash-value life insurance.

Inherited assets.

Royalties.

Or other sources of value.

When you're finished, add everything together.

For the first time, you may be looking at your entire financial life on one page.

That alone can be powerful.

Now Look at What You Owe

Next, list your liabilities.

Mortgage.

Home equity loan.

Car loans.

Credit cards.

Personal loans.

Business debt for which you are personally responsible.

Any other significant obligations.

Retiring with debt isn't automatically bad.

That's important.

There is a tendency to believe that everyone must have absolutely zero debt before retirement.

It certainly can be wonderful to enter retirement debt-free.

But the decision to pay off debt should be evaluated as part of the overall financial plan.

Suppose someone has a mortgage with a relatively low interest rate and paying it off would require withdrawing several hundred thousand dollars from a taxable retirement account.

That withdrawal could potentially create a large tax bill.

It could affect Medicare premiums.

It could reduce future investment flexibility.

It might even push income into a higher tax bracket.

Suddenly, "Should I pay off the mortgage?" isn't quite as simple as it sounded.

That's a theme we're going to revisit many times:

Financial decisions rarely happen in isolation.

Pull one lever, and something else often moves.

Your Net Worth Is Useful—but It Isn't Your Retirement Plan

Once you subtract your liabilities from your assets, you have your approximate net worth.

That's useful information.

But don't make the mistake of assuming net worth tells you whether you're ready to retire.

Imagine two people who each have a net worth of $2 million.

The first has:

$1.6 million invested for retirement and a $400,000 paid-off home.

The second has:

A $1.5 million home, a $300,000 vacation property, and only $200,000 in retirement savings.

Same net worth.

Completely different retirement situation.

Why?

Because your house doesn't automatically produce retirement income.

Neither does a vacation property.

Neither does a collection of cars, land, jewelry, or other assets unless you're willing to sell them, borrow against them, or generate income from them.

That's why retirement planning needs to distinguish between:

What you own

and

What can support your lifestyle.

Those are not always the same thing.

Find Your Future Paychecks

Now let's look at the income that may continue after your career ends.

This is one of the most important parts of your retirement inventory.

Social Security

Start by estimating your Social Security benefit.

Don't simply write down the maximum benefit you've seen advertised somewhere.

Your benefit is based on your own earnings history and claiming decisions.

Write down your estimated benefit at several possible ages.

For example:

Age 62.

Full Retirement Age.

Age 70.

If you're married, do this for both spouses.

Later, we'll spend an entire chapter discussing Social Security strategy because the decision about when to claim can have significant long-term consequences.

For now, we're simply identifying the potential income.

Pensions

If you're fortunate enough to have a pension, gather your benefit estimates.

Don't stop with the monthly amount.

Find out:

When can the pension begin?

Does the benefit change depending on when you retire?

Is there a cost-of-living adjustment?

What survivor options are available?

What happens to the benefit if you die first?

Is retiree healthcare attached to the pension?

Does your spouse need to consent to certain elections?

A statement saying "$4,000 per month" tells us only part of the story.

Other Guaranteed or Predictable Income

You may also have income from:

Rental properties.

Annuities.

Deferred compensation.

Business interests.

Royalties.

Part-time work.

Or other sources.

Write them down.

We're beginning to build your retirement paycheck.

Gross Income Isn't Spendable Income

This seems obvious, but it's one of the most important concepts in retirement planning.

Suppose you determine that you'll have:

$3,500 per month from Social Security.

$3,000 per month from a pension.

$4,000 per month from investment withdrawals.

You might think:

"Great. We have $10,500 a month."

Not exactly.

Some of that money may be taxable.

Some may affect how much of your Social Security becomes taxable.

Some withdrawals could increase your Medicare premiums.

Some income may be taxed differently than other income.

And some accounts may eventually force you to take distributions whether you need the money or not.

That's why I care much more about **spendable income** than gross income.

Your lifestyle isn't funded with gross income.

It's funded with what remains after taxes, healthcare premiums, and other obligations.

Later in this book, we'll spend considerable time discussing how taxes can become one of the biggest controllable expenses in retirement.

For now, remember this:

A dollar in one account isn't necessarily worth exactly the same as a dollar in another account.

A million dollars in a traditional IRA is not the same as a million dollars in a Roth IRA.

Taxes matter.

Know What Kind of Money You Have

Let's take your investment assets and divide them into three broad buckets.

Tax-Deferred Money

This might include traditional:

401(k)s.

403(b)s.

IRAs.

TSP accounts.

And similar retirement plans.

You may have received a tax deduction when the money went in.

The money then grew without annual taxation.

Eventually, however, withdrawals are generally taxable.

You haven't necessarily avoided the tax.

You've postponed it.

Tax-Free Money

Roth IRAs and Roth workplace accounts generally fall into this category when the applicable rules for qualified distributions are satisfied.

You paid taxes before the money went into the account.

Qualified withdrawals can then be received tax-free.

That creates very different planning opportunities in retirement.

Taxable Money

Brokerage accounts, savings accounts, CDs, and similar assets make up another category.

These accounts have their own tax characteristics.

Interest may be taxable.

Dividends may be taxable.

Investment gains may be subject to capital-gains taxes.

But you generally aren't taxed again on the portion representing money you've already contributed.

Each bucket behaves differently.

And one of the most powerful retirement strategies we'll eventually discuss is learning **which bucket to use and when.**

Take Inventory of Your Insurance

Insurance probably isn't the first thing you think about when imagining retirement.

That's understandable.

But remember what we're doing.

We're identifying anything that could either support your retirement plan or threaten it.

Review:

Life insurance.

Long-term care insurance.

Disability insurance if you're still working.

Homeowners coverage.

Umbrella liability coverage.

Health insurance.

And any insurance products connected to your retirement assets.

For life insurance, ask:

Why do I own it?

Who is the beneficiary?

How much coverage is there?

Is it term or permanent?

When does it expire?

Does it have cash value?

Do I still need it?

Again, we're not deciding what to change yet.

We're simply understanding what you have.

Don't Forget the Documents

Some of the most important parts of your financial life don't appear on an investment statement.

Do you have a will?

A durable financial power of attorney?

An advance medical directive?

A trust?

Are the beneficiaries on your retirement accounts current?

What about your life insurance?

Have you named contingent beneficiaries?

If you have a trust, are the appropriate assets actually titled correctly?

These questions become increasingly important as we age.

I've seen situations where people spent significant time and money creating estate documents but never completed the steps necessary to make the plan work as intended.

A beautifully drafted estate plan sitting in a drawer isn't necessarily a completed estate plan.

We'll come back to this later.

For now, add your estate documents to the inventory.

The Beneficiary Audit

> **Provision Should Survive Us**
> *Beneficiary decisions are not paperwork trivia. They are part of providing for people after we are no longer here to explain our intentions. Responsible stewardship includes making those intentions clear.*
> ***Scripture anchor: 1 Timothy 5:8***

Here's a simple exercise that can prevent enormous problems.

Make a list of every account or policy that has a beneficiary designation.

Retirement accounts.

Life insurance.

Annuities.

Certain bank and investment accounts.

Then ask:

Who gets this if I die tonight?

Not who your will says should receive it.

Not who you assume will receive it.

Who is actually listed on the beneficiary form?

Those aren't always the same person.

Divorce.

Remarriage.

Deaths.

Births.

Family changes.

Old beneficiary forms can quietly remain in place for decades.

This is one of those small details that can have very large consequences.

The Retirement Gap

Now we can connect Chapter 1 and Chapter 2.

Chapter 1 asked:

What do you want?

Chapter 2 asks:

What do you have?

The difference between those two is your **retirement gap**.

Suppose you determine that your desired retirement lifestyle requires $10,000 per month after taxes.

Then suppose Social Security and pensions provide the equivalent of $6,000 per month toward that goal.

We now know that some combination of your investments and other resources must support the remaining gap.

That's a much more useful problem to solve than:

"Is $1.5 million enough?"

Enough for what?

Now we know.

The money has a job.

Meet Mark and Lisa Johnson

Let's create a hypothetical couple we'll revisit throughout this book.

We'll call them Mark and Lisa Johnson.

Mark is 62.

Lisa is 60.

They've worked hard, raised two children, paid for college, saved consistently, and are beginning to seriously think about retirement.

Mark would like to retire at 65.

Lisa might retire around the same time.

Their financial picture looks something like this:

Retirement accounts: $1,250,000

Roth accounts: $150,000

Savings and investments: $200,000

Home: $600,000

Mortgage: $125,000

Mark expects Social Security.

Lisa expects Social Security.

Mark also has a small pension.

On paper, things look pretty good.

They have accumulated meaningful assets.

But then I ask them:

"What do you want retirement to look like?"

That's when the conversation changes.

They want to travel extensively during their first ten years.

They want to help pay for their grandchildren's college.

They want to renovate their home.

Mark wants to buy a boat.

Lisa wants to spend a month each winter somewhere warm.

They'd like to give regularly to their church.

And neither wants to become financially dependent on their children later in life.

Suddenly, their account balance isn't the plan.

It's simply the **raw material we're going to use to build the plan.**

Throughout this book, we'll periodically come back to Mark and Lisa.

We'll see how decisions involving Social Security, taxes, investments, healthcare, Roth conversions, estate planning, and retirement income can interact.

Because that's how retirement planning actually works.

Everything connects.

Your Purpose Driven Action Step

Before moving on, gather the following information.

Don't worry if you can't find everything immediately.

Start with what you have.

Assets

Retirement accounts
Roth accounts
Brokerage accounts
Bank accounts
Real estate
Annuities
Business interests
Other significant assets

Liabilities

Mortgage
Home equity loans
Vehicle loans
Credit cards
Business obligations
Other debt

Future Income

Social Security estimates
Pension estimates
Rental income
Annuity income
Part-time employment
Other income

Insurance

Life insurance
Long-term care coverage
Health insurance
Other significant policies

Estate Planning

Will
Trust
Financial power of attorney
Healthcare directive
Beneficiary designations

Then answer three questions.

Question 1

What do we own?

Question 2

What do we owe?

Question 3

What future income can we reasonably expect?

If you can answer those three questions, you've already taken an enormous step forward.

Don't Judge the Starting Point

There is one final thing I want you to remember as you complete this exercise.

Don't judge yourself.

Maybe you're better prepared than you thought.

Wonderful.

Maybe you look at the numbers and realize you're behind.

That's okay too.

Finding out today is better than finding out ten years from now.

A financial plan isn't a report card.

It's a strategy.

And strategies begin with accurate information.

If your retirement gap is larger than expected, we have options.

Maybe you save more.

Maybe you work another year or two.

Maybe you adjust your retirement lifestyle.

Maybe you improve the way your assets are invested.

Maybe you reduce taxes.

Maybe you change your Social Security strategy.

Maybe you use several of those approaches together.

Small changes across several areas can sometimes create a much bigger improvement than one dramatic change.

But we can't determine which changes make sense until we understand the risks standing between you and the retirement you want.

And there are more of them than most people realize.

Market risk.

Inflation.

Taxes.

Longevity.

Healthcare.

Sequence-of-returns risk.

Long-term care.

The death of a spouse.

Poor investment decisions.

And sometimes simply making the right decision at the wrong time.

The purpose isn't to scare you.

It's to prepare you.

Because a good retirement plan doesn't attempt to predict exactly what the next thirty years will look like.

It prepares you for the possibility that they won't look exactly the way you expected.

That's where we're going next.

Chapter 3

What Could Go Wrong?

> **Wisdom Prepares Without Worshiping Fear**
> *Biblical prudence makes room for preparation while refusing to let worry become the organizing principle of life.*
> ***Scripture anchor: Proverbs 22:3; Matthew 6:34***

Nobody wants to begin retirement by asking:

"What could go wrong?"

I understand.

You've spent decades working toward this.

You've saved.

You've invested.

You've raised a family.

You've paid taxes.

You've dealt with bosses, deadlines, traffic, meetings, emails, and alarm clocks.

Retirement is supposed to be the part where you finally get to enjoy yourself.

And it should be.

But there's an important difference between **worrying** about everything that could go wrong and **preparing** for the things that reasonably could.

That's what this chapter is about.

Because a good retirement plan isn't built on the assumption that nothing bad will ever happen.

It's built so that when life doesn't go according to plan, you still have options.

The Retirement You Planned—and the Retirement You Get

Imagine Mark and Lisa Johnson, the couple we met in the last chapter.

They've done well.

They have approximately $1.6 million in retirement and investment assets. They own a valuable home. They'll eventually receive Social Security, and Mark has a pension.

They want to travel.

They want to help their grandchildren.

They want to enjoy their money.

On paper, retirement looks promising.

Now imagine that during Mark's first year of retirement, the stock market falls significantly.

Then inflation remains elevated.

Several years later, one of them develops a health problem.

Eventually, one spouse dies considerably earlier than the other.

The survivor discovers that household income has declined, but many household expenses haven't.

Did their original retirement plan fail?

Not necessarily.

The answer depends on whether the plan anticipated that life might be messy.

That's the purpose of risk planning.

We aren't trying to predict exactly what will happen.

We're asking:

"If this happens, what will we do?"

That is a very different question.

Risk #1: Living Too Long

Let's start with a strange one.

One of the biggest financial risks in retirement is something we're all hoping for:

A long life.

If you knew with certainty that you would die five years after retiring, retirement planning would be relatively easy.

You'd know exactly how long your money needed to last.

But you don't know.

You might live twenty years.

Thirty years.

Forty years.

One spouse may live much longer than the other.

That's what makes longevity risk so important.

Suppose you retire at 65.

If you live to 95, that's thirty years without a traditional paycheck.

Think about how much changed during the previous thirty years.

Prices changed.

Tax laws changed.

Markets changed.

Interest rates changed.

Technology changed.

Healthcare changed.

Your family changed.

Now imagine trying to create a financial strategy today that has to work through another thirty years of uncertainty.

That's retirement planning.

The question isn't simply:

"Do I have enough money to retire?"

It's:

"Can my resources support me if retirement lasts much longer than I expect?"

Don't Plan to the Average

> **Wisdom Leaves Margin**
> *Prudence does not require predicting the exact length of life. It means recognizing uncertainty and leaving reasonable margin. We prepare without pretending that preparation gives us control.*
> ***Scripture anchor: Proverbs 27:1; James 4:13-15***

This is where averages can become dangerous.

Suppose someone tells you the average life expectancy is a certain age.

That's interesting information.

But you're not planning for the average person.

You're planning for **you and your family**.

Family longevity matters.

Health matters.

Lifestyle matters.

And if you're married, the probability that at least one spouse lives to an advanced age can be considerably greater than either spouse's individual probability.

That's why a retirement plan should usually consider what happens if someone lives longer than expected.

Living a long life should be something we celebrate.

Your financial plan simply needs to be prepared to celebrate with you.

Risk #2: Inflation—the Quiet Risk

Inflation doesn't usually arrive like a stock-market crash.

There's no dramatic headline announcing that your retirement plan just lost 30% of its purchasing power.

It happens slowly.

A few dollars here.

A few dollars there.

Groceries cost more.

Insurance premiums rise.

Property taxes increase.

Restaurants get more expensive.

Travel costs more.

Home repairs cost more.

Healthcare costs more.

And eventually you realize that the same amount of money doesn't buy what it used to.

Suppose you retire needing $8,000 per month to maintain your lifestyle.

That may feel like plenty of income today.

But if retirement lasts thirty years, $8,000 won't have the same purchasing power near the end of retirement that it had at the beginning.

That's why simply generating income isn't enough.

We need to think about generating **purchasing power**.

The Dangerous Comfort of Cash

This creates an interesting retirement dilemma.

Many retirees naturally become more conservative.

That makes sense.

When you're working, a market decline may feel frustrating.

When you're retired and withdrawing money from your portfolio, that same decline can feel terrifying.

So some people move large portions of their savings into cash.

Cash feels safe.

The account balance doesn't fluctuate very much.

But safety has more than one definition.

Cash can protect you from short-term market volatility.

It doesn't necessarily protect you from long-term inflation.

If prices continue rising while your money doesn't grow enough to keep pace, you're losing purchasing power even though your statement never shows a loss.

That's why retirement investing isn't about choosing between:

Risky investments and safe investments.

It's about understanding that **different investments protect against different risks.**

We'll spend much more time on that later.

Risk #3: The Market Falls at the Wrong Time

Most investors understand market risk.

Stocks go up.

Stocks go down.

But retirement introduces a particular type of market risk that many people have never encountered before.

It's called **sequence-of-returns risk**.

The concept sounds complicated.

It isn't.

Imagine two retirees.

Both begin retirement with $1 million.

Both withdraw the same amount.

Both ultimately experience the same average investment return over twenty years.

But one experiences strong investment returns early in retirement and poor returns later.

The other experiences poor returns immediately after retiring and strong returns later.

They can end up with dramatically different results.

Why?

Because the second retiree is withdrawing money while the portfolio is down.

That means investments may have to be sold at depressed values to provide income.

Once those shares are sold, they aren't there to participate in the eventual recovery.

This is one of the biggest differences between saving for retirement and **living from your savings**.

The Five Years Before and After Retirement

Think about the ten-year period surrounding retirement:

Five years before.

Retirement day.

Five years after.

That window can be extraordinarily important.

If the market performs well, wonderful.

But suppose the market falls substantially shortly after you retire.

You don't want your only strategy to be:

"I hope it comes back quickly."

Hope is wonderful in life.

It's not a retirement-income strategy.

A well-designed retirement plan should ask in advance:

Where will next year's income come from?

What happens if stocks fall 30%?

What assets could we spend instead?

Could we temporarily reduce withdrawals?

Which expenses are essential and which are discretionary?

Do we have enough liquidity?

These decisions are much easier to make **before** a market decline than during one.

Risk #4: Taxes

Most people don't think of taxes as a retirement risk.

They should.

During your working years, taxes often feel relatively straightforward.

You earn income.

Taxes come out of your paycheck.

You file a return.

Retirement can become much more strategic.

Now your income may come from:

Social Security.

Pensions.

Traditional IRAs.

Roth IRAs.

401(k)s.

Brokerage accounts.

Interest.

Dividends.

Capital gains.

Annuities.

Rental income.

Each source may be taxed differently.

And the source of your next dollar of income can sometimes affect the taxation of other dollars.

The Tax Time Bomb

For decades, many Americans have been encouraged to save in tax-deferred retirement accounts.

And for good reason.

You contribute money.

You may receive a tax deduction.

The money grows without annual taxation.

That's a powerful wealth-building tool.

But remember what we discussed in Chapter 2:

Tax-deferred does not necessarily mean tax-free.

Eventually, the government may require distributions from certain retirement accounts.

Those withdrawals may create taxable income.

For someone who has accumulated a large portion of retirement wealth in tax-deferred accounts, future taxes can become a significant expense.

This doesn't mean traditional retirement accounts are bad.

Far from it.

It means the tax strategy shouldn't stop the day you retire.

In fact, the years between retirement and required distributions can sometimes create some of the most interesting tax-planning opportunities of your lifetime.

We'll devote an entire section of this book to that.

The Widow's Tax Problem

Taxes can become especially important after the death of a spouse.

Imagine a married couple living comfortably in retirement.

Then one spouse dies.

The survivor may lose one Social Security benefit.

A pension may decline depending on the survivor election.

But something else can happen.

Eventually, the surviving spouse may file taxes as a single taxpayer rather than married filing jointly.

Now one person may have:

Many of the same investments.

Many of the same retirement accounts.

A similar house.

Many of the same expenses.

But potentially less favorable tax thresholds.

This is one reason tax planning shouldn't focus solely on:

"How do we pay the least tax this year?"

A better question may be:

"How do we manage taxes intelligently over our lifetime—and potentially our spouse's lifetime?"

Those are not always the same strategy.

Risk #5: Healthcare

Most retirees know healthcare will cost money.

What can be difficult is understanding just how many different expenses fall under the word *healthcare*.

Premiums.

Deductibles.

Copays.

Prescription drugs.

Dental care.

Vision.

Hearing.

Services not fully covered by insurance or Medicare.

And potentially long-term care.

Healthcare needs may also increase during the years when your ability or desire to manage complicated financial decisions decreases.

That creates both a financial risk and a planning risk.

Medicare Isn't Free Healthcare

People sometimes reach age 65 with the impression that Medicare will take care of everything.

It doesn't.

Medicare can provide valuable healthcare coverage, but retirees still need to plan for premiums, supplemental coverage, prescriptions, out-of-pocket expenses, and services Medicare may not fully cover.

Higher-income retirees can also face higher Medicare premiums.

That means certain financial decisions—such as realizing income or taking large retirement-account withdrawals—can have consequences beyond the income-tax return.

Once again:

Everything connects.

Risk #6: Long-Term Care

Long-term care is one of the retirement risks people often prefer not to discuss.

Nobody enjoys imagining themselves needing help bathing, dressing, eating, moving around, or managing everyday life.

But avoiding the conversation doesn't remove the risk.

Long-term care doesn't automatically mean living in a nursing home.

Care might be provided:

At home.

By family.

Through professional caregivers.

In assisted living.

In a memory-care facility.

Or in a skilled nursing facility.

The financial impact can vary dramatically.

So can the emotional impact on a family.

The planning question isn't simply:

"Should I buy long-term care insurance?"

That's only one possible solution.

The broader question is:

"If I need care, what is our plan?"

Who provides it?

Where do I receive it?

How do we pay for it?

What happens financially to my spouse while I'm receiving care?

Those are the questions that matter.

Risk #7: Losing a Spouse

For married couples, retirement planning often begins as a joint exercise.

We will retire.

We will travel.

We will receive Social Security.

We have investments.

But statistically and practically, there is a meaningful possibility that one spouse will eventually spend part of retirement alone.

That's why every retirement plan for a married couple should eventually answer this question:

"What happens financially when the first spouse dies?"

Income may change.

Taxes may change.

Expenses may change.

Insurance may change.

Housing needs may change.

The surviving spouse may suddenly become responsible for financial decisions that the other spouse handled for decades.

That's not simply an estate-planning issue.

It's a retirement-planning issue.

Could Either Spouse Run the Plan?

Here's a question worth asking tonight:

If something happened to you tomorrow, could your spouse explain your financial plan?

Do they know where the accounts are?

Do they know who to call?

Do they understand how income arrives each month?

Do they know which bills are automatically paid?

Do they know where the insurance policies are?

Do they know where your estate documents are?

Do they know the passwords—or at least know how to access the system you've established for them?

And most importantly:

Would they feel confident making financial decisions without you?

If the answer is no, that's a risk we can fix.

Risk #8: Family

> **Generosity Needs Wisdom**
> *Helping family can be one of retirement's greatest joys, but love and wisdom belong together. Assistance should strengthen people where possible rather than quietly endangering the giver's own responsibilities or creating unhealthy dependence.*
> ***Scripture anchor: Proverbs 13:22; 2 Corinthians 9:7***

Sometimes the biggest threat to a retirement plan isn't the stock market.

It's someone you love.

Adult children experience financial problems.

Grandchildren need help.

A family member goes through a divorce.

Someone loses a job.

Someone needs help buying a house.

Parents need financial assistance.

And because you love them, you want to help.

There's nothing wrong with that.

In fact, helping family may be one of the purposes you've intentionally assigned to your money.

But there is an important distinction between:

Helping your family

and

jeopardizing your own financial independence to help your family.

Remember the instructions on an airplane:

Put your own oxygen mask on first.

That's not selfish.

You can't help someone else for very long if you create a financial emergency for yourself.

A good retirement plan can actually make generosity easier because you know how much you can afford to give.

Risk #9: Yourself

> **The Heart Is Part of the Plan**
> *Some retirement risks cannot be diversified away because they arise from fear, greed, impatience, pride, or comparison. A written plan creates financial guardrails; faith and self-awareness help create personal ones.*
> ***Scripture anchor: Proverbs 4:23***

This may be the most underestimated retirement risk of all.

Human behavior.

We like to believe we make financial decisions logically.

We don't.

We're human.

We experience fear.

Greed.

Regret.

Overconfidence.

Panic.

FOMO.

Loss aversion.

And occasionally stubbornness.

When markets rise for several years, people begin believing they'll continue rising.

They take more risk.

Then the market falls.

Fear takes over.

They sell.

Eventually the market recovers.

They wait.

Then they buy back after prices have already risen.

Buy high.

Sell low.

Repeat.

It sounds irrational when written on a page.

It feels very rational when you're watching your life savings fall.

The Investment Statement Test

Imagine opening your retirement statement and seeing that your $1.5 million portfolio is now worth $1.1 million.

How would you feel?

Not theoretically.

Really.

Would you be calm?

Would you call someone?

Would you stop spending?

Would you want to sell?

Would you lie awake wondering whether retirement had been a mistake?

Those answers matter.

Because the mathematically optimal portfolio isn't necessarily the right portfolio if you can't emotionally stay invested in it.

The best strategy is one you can actually follow.

Risk #10: Having No Plan for Change

There is one more risk worth discussing.

Believing your retirement plan is finished.

It's not.

Suppose you create a beautiful plan at age 62.

Then you put it in a binder.

At age 72, you pull it back out.

What are the chances that everything happened exactly as projected?

Probably not very good.

Markets changed.

Tax laws changed.

Interest rates changed.

Your family changed.

Your health changed.

Your goals changed.

Maybe you moved.

Maybe you inherited money.

Maybe you spent more than expected.

Maybe you spent less.

Maybe grandchildren arrived.

Maybe your priorities simply changed.

A retirement plan isn't something you create once.

It's something you **manage**.

The Four Ways to Deal With Risk

Now that we've identified some of the major risks, what do we do about them?

Here's a framework we'll use throughout this book.

There are four basic ways we can respond to financial risk.

1. Avoid It

Sometimes the smartest risk is one you simply don't take.

If losing a particular amount of money would devastate your retirement, maybe you shouldn't expose that money to that particular risk.

Avoiding risk doesn't mean avoiding all investments.

It means recognizing when the potential consequence isn't worth the potential reward.

2. Reduce It

We can't eliminate every risk.

But we can often reduce it.

Diversification may reduce certain investment risks.

Maintaining liquidity can reduce the need to sell investments during bad markets.

Tax planning can reduce future tax exposure.

Estate planning can reduce confusion.

Healthy financial margins can reduce stress.

Small protections can have large effects.

3. Transfer It

Sometimes a risk is too large to comfortably absorb yourself.

That's where insurance can become valuable.

You transfer some financial risk to an insurance company in exchange for a premium or other cost.

Health insurance.

Homeowners insurance.

Life insurance.

Long-term care coverage.

Certain income guarantees.

Insurance isn't designed to make every risk disappear.

Its purpose is often to protect you from a risk whose consequences you don't want to bear alone.

4. Accept It

Finally, some risks should simply be accepted.

You cannot insure against everything.

You shouldn't try.

If an expense would be inconvenient but easily manageable from your resources, self-insuring may make perfect sense.

That's why the goal isn't:

Eliminate risk.

The goal is:

Take the right risks intentionally.

Probability Versus Consequence

Here's another way to think about risk.

Ask two questions:

How likely is this to happen?

and

How damaging would it be if it did?

Something can be unlikely but financially devastating.

Something else can be very likely but financially insignificant.

The second event may not require much planning.

The first one might.

That's why good risk management isn't about worrying equally about everything.

It's about identifying the risks that could permanently change your retirement.

Your Retirement Stress Test

Let's put your plan through a simple stress test.

You don't need sophisticated software.

For now, just ask yourself what you would do in each situation.

Scenario 1: The market falls 30% during your first year of retirement.

Where does your income come from?

Would you need to sell investments?

Scenario 2: Inflation remains higher than expected for several years.

Can your income increase?

Scenario 3: You live to age 100.

Does the plan still work?

Scenario 4: Your spouse dies ten years into retirement.

What income disappears?

How do taxes change?

Scenario 5: One spouse needs several years of care.

Where does the money come from?

Scenario 6: Your adult child asks for $100,000.

Could you help without damaging your own independence?

Scenario 7: Tax rates change.

How much flexibility do you have regarding where your income comes from?

Scenario 8: You become unable or unwilling to manage the finances yourself.

Who takes over?

If some of these questions make you uncomfortable, good.

Not because I want you to worry.

Because we've identified something worth planning for.

Build Guardrails, Not Predictions

One of the biggest mistakes in financial planning is pretending we can predict the future precisely.

We can't.

We can estimate.

We can model.

We can make reasonable assumptions.

But nobody knows exactly what the stock market will return next year.

Nobody knows exactly what tax rates will be twenty years from now.

Nobody knows exactly how long they'll live.

Nobody knows exactly what healthcare will cost.

So rather than building a retirement plan that requires our predictions to be perfect, let's build one with **guardrails**.

If the market falls, we have a response.

If taxes change, we have flexibility.

If inflation rises, part of the portfolio is designed for growth.

If we need care, we know where the resources will come from.

If one spouse dies, the survivor understands the plan.

If circumstances change, we adjust.

That is what financial confidence actually looks like.

Not knowing exactly what will happen.

Knowing that you have a process for responding when it does.

Protect the Purpose

Let's return once again to the central idea of this book.

Why are we managing all these risks?

It isn't because the goal is to protect an account balance.

We're protecting something much more important.

We're protecting the retirement you described in Chapter 1.

The trip to Italy.

The beach house.

The afternoons with grandchildren.

The charitable giving.

The family vacations.

The ability to remain independent.

The ability to help your children.

The ability to sleep at night without wondering whether you'll run out of money.

That's what we're protecting.

Your investments aren't the purpose.

Your Social Security isn't the purpose.

Your pension isn't the purpose.

Your insurance isn't the purpose.

Your tax strategy isn't the purpose.

They're tools.

The purpose is the life those tools are supposed to support.

That's why we identify risks.

That's why we plan.

And that's why our next step is one of the most important transitions in the entire retirement process.

We've defined the life you want.

We've identified the resources you have.

We've considered what could knock the plan off course.

Now we need to answer the question that almost every retiree eventually asks:

"Where will my paycheck come from when I stop working?"

That's where we're going next.

Part II — Creating Your Retirement Paycheck

◆

Chapter 4

Replacing the Paycheck

> **Provision Has a Purpose**
> *Retirement income is not simply a distribution problem. It is the financial structure that supports dignity, family responsibilities, generosity, and the life you hope to live.*
> ***Scripture anchor: 1 Timothy 5:8***

For most of your adult life, retirement planning has been about accumulation.

You worked, earned, saved, invested, and watched your retirement accounts grow.

Maybe slowly at first.

Then, hopefully, faster as the years passed and compounding began doing more of the work.

But retirement changes the assignment.

Now the question isn't:

"How do I grow the account?"

It's:

"How do I turn everything I've accumulated into a reliable paycheck that can last for the rest of my life?"

That is a completely different problem.

And for many retirees, it's the first time they've ever had to solve it.

The Day the Paycheck Stops

Think about your working life.

Your paycheck arrives on schedule.

You may not love everything about your job, but you generally know when the money is coming.

You know approximately how much it will be.

You know which bills it covers.

You know how to budget around it.

Then one day you retire.

No more paycheck.

At least not from your employer.

That change can feel surprisingly unsettling.

A person might have $2 million invested and still feel nervous about spending $6,000 a month.

Why?

Because there's a huge psychological difference between spending income from a paycheck and withdrawing money from a portfolio.

When you're working, the account balance doesn't usually feel like it is shrinking to pay for groceries.

In retirement, it can.

That's why one of the most important jobs of a retirement plan is to replace not just the **income** of a paycheck, but also the **confidence** of a paycheck.

Income Is More Than a Withdrawal Rate

A lot of retirement conversations begin with a withdrawal percentage.

"Can I take 4%?"

"Should I use 3.5%?"

"What about 5%?"

Those are reasonable questions.

But they can cause us to skip over something more important.

Before we ask how much we can withdraw, we should ask:

What kind of income do we need?

There are really two different questions hiding inside one.

Essential Spending Versus Lifestyle Spending

One of the most useful things you can do before retirement is divide your expected expenses into two categories.

Build the Income Floor First

Here's an idea we'll return to throughout this book:

Your essential expenses should have the strongest possible income foundation.

Think of your retirement income as a house.

Before decorating the upstairs, we want a strong foundation.

That foundation may include:

Social Security.

Pensions.

Certain guaranteed income sources.

And potentially other assets designed specifically to support predictable spending.

Let's call this your **income floor**.

The closer your dependable income comes to covering your essential expenses, the less pressure your investment portfolio may have to support your basic standard of living.

That can have enormous psychological value.

Mark and Lisa's Income Floor

Let's return to Mark and Lisa Johnson.

They want approximately $10,000 per month after taxes to support the retirement lifestyle they've described.

After reviewing their expenses, they determine that about $6,500 per month represents essential spending.

The remaining $3,500 supports:

Travel, dining out, entertainment, gifts, home projects, and other lifestyle expenses.

Now let's suppose their future income includes:

Mark's pension.

Mark's Social Security.

Lisa's Social Security.

Together, once fully in place, those sources may cover a substantial portion of their essential spending.

That changes the planning conversation.

Instead of saying:

"We need our investments to produce $120,000 every year no matter what happens."

We might discover that the portfolio only needs to fill part of the gap.

And some of that gap represents spending they have the flexibility to adjust temporarily.

That's a much stronger position.

Think in Layers

Retirement income often works better when we think in layers rather than relying on a single source.

Layer 1: Dependable Income

This might include: Social Security, pensions, certain annuity income, dependable rental income, and other predictable lifetime income.

This layer helps create the income floor.

Layer 2: Near-Term Spending

This is money you expect to need in the relatively near future.

That might include cash, money-market funds, short-term bonds, and other lower-volatility assets.

The purpose isn't necessarily maximum return.

The purpose is availability.

Layer 3: Long-Term Growth

This is the portion of your money that may need to grow for the future.

Remember: retirement could last thirty years or more.

We still need to think about inflation.

We still need growth.

We still need resources for the person you may be twenty years from now.

This layer may contain more growth-oriented investments.

The key is understanding that **not every dollar has the same job**.

Don't Make Every Dollar Fight the Same Battle

Imagine putting every dollar of your retirement savings into one investment strategy.

Now that one portfolio has to do everything.

It needs to provide next month's income.

Protect against market declines.

Beat inflation.

Provide emergency cash.

Fund healthcare.

Grow for twenty years.

And eventually leave money to your family.

That's a lot to ask of one pool of money.

A more intentional approach asks:

What is this money for?

Money needed next year may have a different investment objective than money you may not touch for twenty years.

Money intended for grandchildren may have a different job than money intended to pay the electric bill.

Once you understand the job, it becomes much easier to think about the appropriate strategy.

The Retirement Paycheck System

Let's make this practical.

Suppose you need $9,000 each month deposited into your checking account.

Some of that income may arrive automatically.

Social Security may be deposited every month.

A pension may arrive monthly.

Maybe rental income arrives monthly.

Then your investments fill whatever gap remains.

Instead of randomly withdrawing money whenever bills are due, you can create a **retirement paycheck system**.

For example, your investment account might automatically transfer a fixed amount to checking every month.

Now retirement starts feeling more familiar.

Money arrives, bills are paid, and you have a routine while the investments work in the background.

This may sound like a small operational detail.

It isn't.

Behavior matters.

People often feel more comfortable spending money when the system resembles the paycheck structure they've used their entire adult lives.

The Income Gap

Here's the basic retirement-income equation.

Start with the lifestyle you want.

Then subtract dependable income.

What's left is the amount your portfolio and other resources must provide.

Suppose a couple wants $9,000 per month after taxes.

Their Social Security and pension eventually provide $5,500 per month toward that goal.

Their portfolio needs to help fund the difference.

That difference is the **income gap**.

Once we know the gap, several questions become easier to answer.

How much of the portfolio needs to produce current income?

How much can remain invested for growth?

How much cash should be available?

How much flexibility does the couple have during difficult markets?

Where should withdrawals come from?

Those are the decisions that create a retirement-income strategy.

Spending Principal Isn't Failure

This is an important psychological hurdle.

Many retirees say:

"I don't want to touch the principal."

I understand why.

For decades, you've been trained to protect the account balance.

Spending principal can feel like moving backward.

But consider why you accumulated the money in the first place.

If someone saves $2 million for retirement and then refuses to use any of it to support retirement, what exactly was the purpose of saving it?

Certainly, we need to protect against longevity.

We may want to leave an inheritance.

We may need money for future healthcare.

But spending a thoughtfully planned portion of your assets isn't necessarily a failure.

It may be exactly what the plan was designed to do.

Remember:

The account balance isn't the goal.

The life the account supports is the goal.

Give Yourself Permission to Spend

> **Enjoyment Can Be Stewardship Too**
> *Scripture does not present every dollar spent on enjoyment as a dollar wasted. Ecclesiastes recognizes the ability to enjoy the fruits of our labor as a gift. Responsible spending can honor the purpose for which decades of saving were undertaken.*
> ***Scripture anchor: Ecclesiastes 5:18-20***

Here's a problem that doesn't receive enough attention.

Some retirees are financially capable of spending more than they do.

They've built a strong plan.

Their income is secure.

Their assets are substantial.

Their goals are funded.

And they're still afraid to spend.

Why?

Because retirement creates uncertainty.

"What if the market crashes?"

"What if I live to 100?"

"What if healthcare gets expensive?"

"What if I need the money later?"

These are legitimate concerns.

But without a plan, every purchase can feel dangerous.

A good plan can provide something that is hard to quantify:

permission.

Permission to take the trip, help the grandchildren, buy the boat, and enjoy the money.

Not recklessly.

Purposefully.

Because the plan has already accounted for the future.

Give Yourself Permission to Say No

> **Contentment Protects the Plan**
> *Financial independence is not the ability to buy everything. It is the freedom to decide what is enough. Contentment can protect retirement from lifestyle inflation, comparison, and obligations that do not serve what matters most.*
> ***Scripture anchor: 1 Timothy 6:6-8***

The opposite is also true.

A good retirement-income plan may show you when an expense is too large.

Maybe the second home creates too much financial pressure.

Maybe gifting $200,000 to a child would materially reduce your own security.

Maybe retiring three years earlier would require compromises you don't want to make.

That isn't planning failure.

That's planning doing its job.

A good financial plan shouldn't tell you what you want to hear.

It should help you understand the consequences of your choices.

Then you decide which tradeoffs are worth making.

Flexible Spending Is a Superpower

Let's return to sequence-of-returns risk.

Suppose the market falls dramatically during the first few years of retirement.

A retiree who needs every dollar of their planned withdrawals may have limited options.

But another retiree may be able to say:

"This year we'll skip the big trip."

"We'll postpone replacing the car."

"We'll take $10,000 less from the portfolio."

That flexibility can significantly reduce pressure on the investments during a bad market.

You don't need every expense to be flexible.

You just need enough flexibility to create options.

That's why separating essential and lifestyle spending is so valuable.

Build a Cash Reserve With a Purpose

How much cash should you have in retirement?

There's no perfect answer.

But the decision should be intentional.

Cash may serve several jobs:

Cash can cover emergency expenses, near-term spending, large planned purchases, a buffer during market downturns, and something less measurable but equally valuable: peace of mind.

Suppose you know you'll need $40,000 for a home renovation next year.

That money probably shouldn't depend on what the stock market does over the next twelve months.

Likewise, money needed for your ordinary living expenses soon after retirement may deserve a different risk profile than money intended for twenty years later.

Cash isn't there because we're afraid to invest.

It's there because we've assigned it a specific job.

Create a Spending Reserve

Some retirees may find it useful to maintain a designated spending reserve.

Imagine having enough lower-volatility assets to cover a period of planned portfolio withdrawals.

If the market performs well, you can periodically refill the reserve.

If the market falls sharply, you may be able to temporarily rely on the reserve rather than selling growth investments at depressed prices.

This doesn't eliminate market risk.

Nothing does.

But it can create flexibility.

And flexibility is one of the most valuable assets you can have in retirement.

A Paycheck Should Be Reviewed

When you were working, your salary probably changed over time.

Your retirement paycheck may need to change too.

At least once a year, review:

How much are we spending?

Has inflation changed our needs?

Did the portfolio grow?

Did the portfolio decline?

Has our tax situation changed?

Has our health changed?

Are we traveling more?

Are we traveling less?

Are we helping family?

Did we inherit money?

Do we have a major purchase coming?

Retirement income shouldn't be placed on autopilot for thirty years.

It should be managed.

Mark and Lisa Build Their Paycheck

Let's put the pieces together for Mark and Lisa.

Their desired retirement lifestyle is approximately $10,000 per month after taxes.

They identify roughly $6,500 of that as essential.

The remaining $3,500 is lifestyle spending.

Their future Social Security and pension benefits will create part of their income floor.

Their portfolio must provide the remaining income.

Instead of putting all $1.6 million into one retirement-income investment, they begin thinking in jobs.

Some money will provide liquidity and near-term spending.

Some will produce income.

Some will remain invested for long-term growth.

Some will provide tax flexibility.

Some may eventually be intended for their children.

Now we aren't simply managing a portfolio.

We're building a **retirement-income system**.

That's a very different mindset.

Your Purpose Driven Action Step

Take out the answers you created in the previous chapters.

Now complete the following exercise.

Step 1: Determine Your Desired Monthly Spending

How much would you like to spend each month in retirement?

Use an after-tax number if possible.

Don't worry about whether the number is affordable yet.

Start with the lifestyle.

Step 2: Separate Essential and Lifestyle Expenses

How much of that amount represents expenses that must be paid?

How much represents discretionary lifestyle spending?

Step 3: List Your Dependable Income

Social Security.

Pensions.

Annuities.

Rental income.

Other predictable income.

Step 4: Calculate the Income Gap

How much remains after dependable income?

That's the amount your portfolio or other resources may need to support.

Step 5: Identify Your Flexibility

If markets were down significantly for a year or two, which expenses could you temporarily reduce?

Which could not?

Step 6: Identify Large Future Expenses

Travel.

Vehicles.

Home renovations.

Second homes.

Family gifts.

Weddings.

College funding.

Put approximate dates and amounts next to them.

Now your retirement income starts becoming much more specific.

Income Is a System, Not a Product

This may be one of the most important ideas in this chapter.

There is no single retirement product that solves every retirement-income problem.

Not a stock.

Not a bond.

Not an annuity.

Not a mutual fund.

Not a dividend strategy.

Not Social Security.

Not a pension.

The strongest retirement-income plans often combine several tools.

Each one solves a different part of the problem.

The goal is to create the right combination for **your** life.

That's why we'll now begin examining those tools individually.

And we'll start with one of the most important retirement-income decisions most Americans will ever make.

It is a benefit you've paid into for decades.

It may provide income for the rest of your life.

It may affect your spouse.

And the decision about when to begin receiving it can potentially influence hundreds of thousands of dollars over a lifetime.

Social Security.

The question sounds simple:

"When should I take it?"

The answer often isn't.

And that's where we're going next.

Chapter 5

Social Security — More Than a Break-Even Calculation

> **People Before Optimization**
> *A claiming decision can affect a spouse and survivor for decades. The highest personal check is not automatically the most responsible household decision.*
> ***Scripture anchor: Philippians 2:4***

Few retirement decisions generate more opinions than Social Security.

Ask ten people when you should claim your benefit and you may get ten different answers.

"Take it at 62. You never know how long you're going to live."

"Wait until 70. The benefit gets bigger."

"Take it as soon as you retire."

"Spend your investments first and let Social Security grow."

"I paid into it my whole life. I want my money back."

Some of those statements may be perfectly reasonable for a particular person.

None of them is a Social Security strategy.

Because the question isn't simply:

"When should I take Social Security?"

The better question is:

"How should Social Security fit into my overall retirement-income plan?"

And for married couples, there's an even more important question:

"How should our two Social Security benefits work together—both while we're alive and after one of us is gone?"

That's where Social Security planning becomes much more interesting.

Social Security Is More Than a Monthly Check

Let's start with the basic idea.

During your working years, you pay Social Security taxes on covered earnings.

Your eventual retirement benefit is based largely on your earnings history and the age at which you begin receiving benefits.

Generally, you have choices.

You may be able to begin retirement benefits as early as age 62.

You have a Full Retirement Age, often abbreviated FRA, based on your year of birth.

And you may delay claiming beyond Full Retirement Age, potentially increasing your retirement benefit up to age 70.

That gives us several possible claiming ages.

But those choices shouldn't be evaluated only by comparing monthly checks.

Social Security has characteristics that can make it unusually valuable inside a retirement plan.

It can provide income for life.

Benefits receive cost-of-living adjustments when applicable under Social Security rules.

And for married couples, Social Security includes spousal and survivor provisions.

That last feature is especially important.

Because when we make a Social Security decision for one spouse, we may also be making a decision that affects the other spouse many years later.

The Temptation to Claim at 62

There's something psychologically attractive about age 62.

You become eligible and think:

"Why wouldn't I take it?"

Maybe you've paid Social Security taxes for forty years.

Maybe you're retiring.

Maybe you'd rather receive the money while you're young enough to enjoy it.

And there's always that uncomfortable thought:

"What if I wait and die before I get my money back?"

That's understandable.

But claiming early generally means accepting a permanently reduced retirement benefit compared with waiting until Full Retirement Age.

And delaying beyond Full Retirement Age can generally increase the worker's retirement benefit through delayed retirement credits until age 70.

So the decision isn't simply whether you want money now.

You're choosing between:

More checks sooner

and

Potentially larger checks later.

Neither is automatically right.

The Break-Even Question

One of the most common ways people evaluate Social Security is through a break-even analysis.

The idea is simple.

Suppose claiming early gives you several years of payments before you would have received anything under a delayed strategy.

If you wait, however, your future monthly benefit is larger.

Eventually, the cumulative amount received under the delayed strategy may catch up with the cumulative amount received under the early strategy.

That's the break-even point.

People often ask:

"How long do I have to live before waiting pays off?"

That's useful information.

But it isn't enough.

A break-even calculation treats Social Security primarily as an investment.

Social Security isn't simply an investment account.

It's also a form of longevity protection.

The longer you live, the more valuable a larger lifetime income stream may become.

And when you're married, the analysis can become even more important because the decision may affect the surviving spouse.

Stop Thinking About Two Separate Benefits

This is where I want married couples to think differently.

Suppose a husband and wife each qualify for Social Security.

One spouse has a substantially larger benefit than the other.

It's tempting to evaluate them independently:

"When should you claim yours?"

"When should I claim mine?"

But retirement isn't lived on two separate spreadsheets.

The couple has one household.

One lifestyle.

One retirement-income plan.

And eventually, in many marriages, there will be one surviving spouse.

So rather than asking when each person should claim independently, consider:

"How can we coordinate these two benefits to support the household throughout both of our lives?"

That may lead to a very different strategy.

Staging Social Security Benefits

One strategy worth considering for some married couples is what I'll call **staging Social Security**.

The concept is relatively straightforward.

Suppose one spouse has the smaller Social Security retirement benefit.

The other spouse has the larger benefit.

Rather than having both spouses claim at the same time, the couple may consider having the spouse with the smaller benefit begin earlier while the spouse with the larger benefit delays.

Why?

Because we're trying to accomplish two things.

First, the smaller benefit begins providing household income sooner.

That may reduce the amount that needs to be withdrawn from investments during the early retirement years.

Second—and perhaps more importantly—the larger benefit has additional time to grow under the Social Security claiming rules, potentially creating a much larger lifetime benefit.

That larger benefit may eventually serve two people.

First the higher-earning spouse.

And potentially later, the surviving spouse.

Think About the Survivor First

> **Love Changes the Math**
> *The best Social Security decision is not always the one that maximizes one person's lifetime benefit. Marriage can require looking first at the household and especially at the person who may live longest with the consequences of today's choice.*
> ***Scripture anchor: Philippians 2:4***

This is one of the most important Social Security concepts in this book.

When one spouse dies, the surviving spouse generally does not continue receiving both full Social Security benefits indefinitely.

Under the survivor-benefit rules, the survivor may generally receive a benefit based on the deceased spouse's record if that produces a higher benefit, subject to the applicable claiming rules.

In practical terms, the household often goes from two Social Security checks to one. A surviving spouse who qualifies for both a survivor benefit and a retirement benefit generally does not receive the two full benefits added together; Social Security pays the applicable combined amount under its rules, and survivor claiming age can affect the amount.

Which check would you rather keep?

Usually the larger one.

That's why delaying the larger benefit can sometimes be thought of as building a **future safety net for the surviving spouse**.

We're not merely maximizing the higher earner's Social Security.

We're potentially increasing the income that could remain after the first spouse dies.

That is an entirely different way of looking at the decision.

Mark and Lisa Stage Their Benefits

Let's return to Mark and Lisa.

Suppose Mark has the larger Social Security benefit.

Lisa's benefit is considerably smaller.

They're both healthy and have sufficient retirement resources.

They could both claim Social Security relatively early.

That would give them more income today.

But let's look beyond today.

Instead, they consider a staged approach.

Lisa claims her smaller retirement benefit earlier.

That income begins helping support their household.

Meanwhile, Mark delays his larger retirement benefit.

As Mark waits—subject to the Social Security rules governing his situation—his eventual retirement benefit increases.

Later, Mark begins receiving his larger benefit.

Now let's move the story forward.

Mark dies first.

Lisa is still alive.

Their household expenses decline somewhat.

But they don't fall in half.

Lisa still has:

Property taxes.

Utilities.

Home maintenance.

Insurance.

Transportation.

Healthcare.

Food.

Travel.

And many of the same basic expenses they had as a couple.

But the household no longer receives two Social Security benefits.

This is where the earlier decision becomes important.

Because Mark delayed his larger benefit, the Social Security income potentially available to Lisa as a surviving spouse may be greater than it would have been if Mark had claimed his retirement benefit earlier, assuming the applicable survivor-benefit requirements are met.

The decision Mark and Lisa made years earlier wasn't simply:

"Should Mark wait for a bigger check?"

It was:

"How much dependable lifetime income do we want available to whichever one of us lives the longest?"

That's retirement planning.

The Survivor Income Gap

Remember the income floor we built in Chapter 4?

Now imagine one spouse dies.

We need to build it again.

Suppose a couple receives:

Two Social Security benefits.

A pension.

Portfolio withdrawals.

Then one spouse dies.

One Social Security benefit disappears.

Maybe the pension changes.

Taxes may change.

Some expenses decline.

Others barely move.

That creates what we can call the **survivor income gap**.

Every married couple should understand this number.

Ask:

If I die first, what happens to my spouse's income?

Then reverse the question:

If my spouse dies first, what happens to mine?

If the answer reveals a significant shortfall, you may have identified one of the most important risks in the retirement plan.

Social Security Can Be Longevity Insurance

Think about what happens if you live much longer than expected.

Your investments have to last longer.

Inflation has more time to affect your purchasing power.

Healthcare expenses may increase.

You have fewer remaining opportunities to return to work and rebuild savings.

That makes dependable lifetime income increasingly valuable as you age.

This is why delaying Social Security can sometimes be viewed as purchasing additional longevity protection.

You're giving up income during one period in exchange for potentially greater income later.

That doesn't make delaying automatically correct.

Someone with poor health, limited resources, or an immediate need for income may have very good reasons to claim earlier.

But the decision should be intentional.

"But What If I Die Early?"

This is the objection I hear frequently.

"If I wait until 70 and die at 71, I made a terrible decision."

Maybe.

But let's examine what we're really saying.

If you're single and have no dependents affected by the decision, longevity and break-even considerations may play a particularly important role.

But if you're married, your death may not end the financial impact of your claiming decision.

Your spouse may still be here.

If you were the higher earner and your claiming decision helped establish a larger survivor benefit, delaying may still have accomplished something important.

You weren't only planning for your lifetime.

You were planning for **the longer of two lifetimes**.

That's why married couples should be careful about making Social Security decisions independently.

There Is No Universal Best Age

If someone tells you that everyone should claim Social Security at 62, be cautious.

If someone tells you everyone should wait until 70, be equally cautious.

Neither statement reflects how retirement planning actually works.

The appropriate claiming strategy may depend on:

Health.

Longevity expectations.

Marital status.

The age difference between spouses.

Relative benefit amounts.

Employment.

Pensions.

Taxes.

Investment assets.

Cash-flow needs.

Survivor needs.

Estate goals.

Risk tolerance.

And the rest of the retirement plan.

That's why two people with identical Social Security benefits may reasonably make different claiming decisions.

When Specialized Social Security Knowledge Helps

Social Security rules can be surprisingly complicated.

Retirement benefits are only one part of the system.

There are also rules involving:

Spousal benefits.

Survivor benefits.

Divorced spouses.

Widows and widowers.

Employment while receiving benefits.

Taxation.

Disability.

Dependent benefits.

And coordination with other retirement decisions.

For consumers who want professional assistance, it can be useful to work with someone who has made Social Security planning a specific area of study.

There are professional education programs and designations focused on Social Security, including the **National Social Security Advisor (NSSA)** designation and the **Registered Social Security Analyst (RSSA)** designation.

A designation alone should never replace good judgment, experience, or comprehensive financial planning.

But specialized education can be valuable because Social Security decisions often involve far more than simply choosing an age on a chart.

When interviewing a financial professional, don't be afraid to ask:

"What specific training do you have in Social Security planning?"

That's a fair question.

Your Purpose Driven Action Step

Before deciding when to claim Social Security, gather the information necessary to answer these questions.

1. What is my estimated retirement benefit at 62?

2. What is my benefit at Full Retirement Age?

3. What is my estimated benefit at 70?

4. What are my spouse's corresponding benefits?

5. Which spouse has the larger benefit?

6. What happens to our retirement income if I die first?

7. What happens if my spouse dies first?

8. Could claiming the smaller benefit earlier and delaying the larger benefit improve our long-term income security?

9. How would different claiming ages affect withdrawals from our investment portfolio?

10. How might taxes affect the decision?

11. Will either of us continue working while receiving benefits?

12. What happens if one of us lives to 95—or 100?

Now we're asking much better questions than:

"When do I get my money back?"

Protect the Last Survivor

There is one final concept I want married couples to remember.

When you're both alive, you have each other.

You may have two Social Security benefits.

Two people making decisions.

Possibly two pensions.

Shared responsibilities.

Then one day, one of you may be gone.

The survivor may be older.

They may be less comfortable managing investments.

They may have fewer opportunities to correct financial mistakes.

They may have increasing healthcare needs.

And they may have less income.

One of the greatest acts of financial planning within a marriage is creating a plan that doesn't merely work while you're both alive.

It continues taking care of the person you love after you're gone.

Sometimes delaying the larger Social Security benefit can be part of creating that protection.

Not because age 70 is magically the right answer.

Not because everyone should delay.

But because the largest Social Security benefit in a household can represent something more important than today's income.

It can become part of the surviving spouse's financial safety net.

And that's exactly how we should evaluate retirement decisions throughout this book.

Not individually.

Not in isolation.

Not simply according to which choice produces the biggest number on a spreadsheet.

But according to one question:

Which decision gives us the best opportunity to protect the life—and the people—that matter most?

That's Purpose Driven Retirement.

And Social Security is only one piece of that income floor.

For many retirees, there is another.

A pension.

And just like Social Security, the biggest pension check isn't always the best pension decision.

Sometimes the most important check is the one that continues after you're gone.

Other Social Security Rules Still Matter

Spousal, survivor, divorced-spouse, widow and widower, work-and-earnings, taxation, and Medicare interactions can all change the answer. The purpose of this chapter is not to turn you into a Social Security technician. It is to make sure you understand that a claiming decision should be made with the entire household in view.

Don't guess. Verify the rules that apply to your situation before you file.

Chapter 6

The Pension Decision — It's Not Just About the Biggest Check

> **Protect the Household**
> *A pension election illustrates a recurring stewardship principle: sometimes accepting less for ourselves can create greater protection for someone we love.*
> ***Scripture anchor: 1 Timothy 5:8***

If you have a pension, congratulations.

You're becoming part of a smaller group of Americans who will enter retirement with a traditional source of lifetime income.

That can be incredibly valuable.

A pension can help pay the mortgage.

Buy groceries.

Cover utilities.

Fund travel.

And perhaps most importantly, provide income without requiring you to sell investments every month.

But having a pension also creates one of the most important decisions you may ever make.

And sometimes that decision is permanent.

You may be presented with several options:

A larger monthly payment for your lifetime.

A smaller monthly payment that continues partially or fully to your spouse after your death.

A lump-sum distribution.

Different survivor percentages.

Different starting dates.

Different cost-of-living provisions.

And potentially different healthcare consequences.

At first glance, the choice can seem obvious.

"Which option pays me the most money?"

That's usually the wrong question.

The better question is:

"Which option does the best job of protecting our retirement plan?"

A Pension Is an Income Asset

People tend to think about assets as things with account balances.

A 401(k).

An IRA.

A brokerage account.

A savings account.

But a pension is also an asset.

It simply looks different.

Instead of giving you a large account balance, the pension may provide a stream of income.

Imagine someone retires with a pension paying $5,000 per month for life.

That's $60,000 per year.

Producing that amount of dependable lifetime income from an investment portfolio could require a substantial amount of capital.

So don't dismiss a pension because you can't see an account balance on a statement.

Its economic value may be significant.

And because it may provide income for life, the decision about how you elect that pension deserves serious attention.

The Seduction of the Biggest Check

Imagine you're retiring and your pension administrator gives you two simplified choices.

Option A

$5,000 per month for your life.

When you die, the pension stops.

Option B

$4,500 per month for your life.

If you die first, your spouse continues receiving $4,500 per month for life.

Which one looks better?

Option A gives you another $500 every month.

That's $6,000 per year.

It can be tempting to say:

"Why would I voluntarily take less money?"

But that $500 difference isn't simply money you're giving up.

You're purchasing something.

Survivor protection.

The real question becomes:

Is the survivor protection worth the reduction in income?

Now we have something useful to analyze.

What Happens If You Die Next Year?

Whenever someone is considering a pension election, I like to move the timeline.

Don't begin by assuming you'll both live thirty years.

Ask:

"What happens if I die one year after retiring?"

Suppose you chose the single-life pension because it provided the largest monthly benefit.

You die.

The pension stops.

What happens to your spouse?

Maybe they're financially secure.

Perhaps they have their own pension.

Perhaps they have substantial investments.

Maybe Social Security and other income easily cover their needs.

In that case, choosing the single-life option might deserve consideration.

But perhaps your pension represents 40% of the household's dependable retirement income.

Now your death creates an enormous income gap.

The extra $500 per month you enjoyed while alive suddenly looks much less important.

Then Ask the Opposite Question

Now suppose you choose the joint-and-survivor option.

You and your spouse both live another thirty years.

You received $500 less every month during that entire period.

Would you regret the decision?

Maybe.

Maybe not.

That's why pension planning isn't about automatically choosing the survivor option either.

We're evaluating tradeoffs.

What does the protection cost?

What risk does it protect against?

What other assets are available?

How healthy are both spouses?

How much income does each spouse have independently?

What happens to Social Security after the first death?

What does the surviving spouse actually need?

Good planning requires both sides of the analysis.

Single Life Versus Joint and Survivor

Pension terminology varies from plan to plan, but many plans provide some version of these choices.

Single-Life Benefit

You receive income for your lifetime.

When you die, payments generally stop.

This option often provides the largest monthly benefit.

Joint-and-Survivor Benefit

You accept a smaller monthly benefit.

In exchange, some or all of the pension continues to your designated spouse or survivor after your death according to the plan's rules.

The survivor percentage may vary.

For example:

50%.

75%.

100%.

Other structures may be available.

Generally, the greater the survivor protection, the greater the reduction to the initial pension benefit.

But the actual options depend entirely on the pension plan.

Don't Analyze the Pension by Itself

Remember our rule:

Everything connects.

Let's bring Social Security back into the conversation.

Suppose Mark has:

The larger Social Security benefit.

A pension.

Lisa has:

A smaller Social Security benefit.

No pension.

While they're both alive, the household may receive:

Mark's Social Security.

Lisa's Social Security.

Mark's pension.

Portfolio income.

Then Mark dies.

Lisa may eventually receive the larger applicable Social Security benefit rather than continuing to receive both full benefits.

If Mark chose a single-life pension, that income may disappear too.

Suddenly Lisa could lose:

One Social Security benefit.

And the entire pension.

That's why we don't make the Social Security decision on Tuesday and the pension decision on Thursday as though they have nothing to do with one another.

They are both part of Lisa's future income floor.

Build the Survivor Paycheck Before You Retire

Here's an exercise every married couple with a pension should complete.

Create two columns.

The first is:

Income While We're Both Alive

The second is:

Income After the First Death

List everything.

Social Security.

Pension.

Investment withdrawals.

Annuity income.

Rental income.

Other dependable income.

Then calculate what disappears.

Now do something else.

Estimate what expenses disappear.

This is where people sometimes make a dangerous assumption.

They think:

"If one of us dies, our expenses will be cut in half."

Usually not.

The house doesn't become half as expensive.

Property taxes don't fall by 50%.

The electric bill doesn't disappear.

Homeowners insurance doesn't get cut in half.

A car may still be necessary.

Healthcare is still necessary.

Groceries decline, but not by half.

Travel may change.

Some discretionary spending may fall.

But many core household expenses remain.

That's why the survivor's income may fall much faster than the survivor's expenses.

Pension and Social Security: Build Them Together

This is where the staged Social Security strategy from the last chapter becomes even more powerful.

Suppose the lower Social Security benefit is claimed earlier.

The higher benefit is delayed.

At the same time, the couple elects an appropriate pension survivor option.

Now we're constructing the surviving spouse's income floor intentionally.

Maybe the survivor eventually receives:

The larger Social Security benefit.

A percentage of the pension.

Portfolio income.

Now compare that with another couple who simply:

Claimed both Social Security benefits as soon as possible.

Chose the largest single-life pension.

They may have maximized today's income.

But they may have unintentionally created a much weaker financial position for the surviving spouse.

More income today isn't always more security tomorrow.

What About the Lump Sum?

Some pension plans offer another choice.

Instead of receiving monthly pension income, you may be offered a lump sum.

Perhaps:

$800,000 today.

Or:

$5,000 per month for life.

Now we have a very different decision.

People sometimes look at the lump sum and immediately think:

"I'd rather control my own money."

That's understandable.

The lump sum offers advantages.

Control.

Liquidity.

Potential investment growth.

Potential inheritance.

Flexibility.

But the pension may offer something the lump sum does not automatically provide:

Guaranteed lifetime income under the terms of the plan.

Neither choice is automatically better.

Questions to Ask Before Taking the Lump Sum

If you're considering a lump-sum pension option, ask:

How healthy am I?

How healthy is my spouse?

How long might we reasonably live?

How financially strong is the pension plan?

What guarantees or protections apply?

Does the pension have a cost-of-living adjustment?

What survivor benefits are available?

What investment return would the lump sum need to generate?

How much would we need to withdraw annually?

How comfortable are we managing investment risk?

How important is liquidity?

How important is leaving an inheritance?

What are the tax consequences?

Could taking the lump sum affect other parts of the retirement plan?

Only after answering those questions can you make a meaningful comparison.

Don't Compare a Pension to an Average Market Return

Here's a mistake I see in pension comparisons.

Someone says:

"My pension is paying the equivalent of 6%, but I think I can earn 8% in the stock market. I'll take the lump sum."

Those aren't equivalent numbers.

The pension payment isn't simply an investment return.

Part of the payment may economically represent return of principal.

It may include longevity pooling.

It may provide lifetime guarantees.

The stock market return isn't guaranteed.

And an average return doesn't tell you the order in which those returns will occur.

Remember sequence-of-returns risk?

It matters.

If you take the lump sum and the market declines substantially during your first few years of retirement while you're withdrawing money, your experience may look very different from the average return printed in a hypothetical illustration.

The Pension Maximization Strategy

You may encounter a strategy sometimes referred to as **pension maximization**.

The concept typically works like this.

Instead of electing a reduced joint-and-survivor pension, the retiree chooses the larger single-life pension.

Then some of the additional pension income is used to purchase life insurance intended to provide money to the surviving spouse if the pensioner dies first.

Conceptually, it can sound attractive.

Take the larger pension.

Use part of the difference to buy insurance.

Potentially leave the spouse a lump sum.

But this strategy requires careful analysis.

Life Insurance Isn't Automatically a Substitute for a Survivor Pension

If you're evaluating pension maximization, ask:

Is the retiree insurable?

What does the life insurance cost?

Is the policy guaranteed?

How long are premiums required?

Could premiums increase?

What happens if the policy lapses?

How financially strong is the insurer?

How much death benefit is needed?

Would the death benefit realistically replace the lost pension?

What investment return would the surviving spouse need?

How long might the survivor live?

Does the pension include cost-of-living adjustments?

What happens if the insurance company changes?

What happens if circumstances change twenty years from now?

Pension maximization can be appropriate in some situations.

It can also be disastrous if it's sold as a simple trick to "get the bigger pension."

The insurance and pension need to be evaluated together.

Cost-of-Living Adjustments Matter

Suppose you're comparing two pensions.

Both pay $4,000 per month.

One includes some form of cost-of-living adjustment.

The other doesn't.

Those are not economically identical benefits.

Remember inflation.

If your pension remains exactly $4,000 per month for thirty years while prices continue rising, its purchasing power can decline significantly.

A pension with inflation protection may therefore be worth considerably more than the initial monthly payment suggests.

When reviewing a pension, always ask:

Does this benefit increase?

If so:

How?

When?

Is there a cap?

Is the increase guaranteed?

Does the survivor benefit receive the same adjustment?

Details matter.

The Starting Date Matters Too

Some pensions provide different benefits depending on when you begin.

Retire earlier?

Smaller benefit.

Work longer?

Larger benefit.

Sometimes substantially larger.

That means your retirement-date decision can affect more than one thing simultaneously.

Another year of work might:

Increase the pension.

Increase Social Security.

Allow another year of retirement contributions.

Reduce the number of years your portfolio must support.

Provide another year of employer health insurance.

Give investments another year to potentially grow.

One additional year can sometimes improve a retirement plan from several directions at once.

That doesn't mean you should automatically work longer.

Remember the purpose.

If you can afford to retire and another year at work would make you miserable, the bigger pension may not be worth the lost year of freedom.

Financial planning isn't about maximizing every dollar.

It's about making informed tradeoffs.

Federal Employees: A Different Level of Complexity

Federal employees deserve special mention.

The federal retirement system can involve several interconnected benefits, potentially including:

FERS or, for some longer-tenured employees, CSRS.

The Thrift Savings Plan.

Social Security.

Federal Employees Health Benefits.

Federal Employees' Group Life Insurance.

Survivor elections.

Sick-leave credit.

Special retirement provisions for certain occupations.

And other rules that can affect the retirement decision.

A federal employee may be making decisions involving several of these benefits at the same time.

For example, a survivor election may affect not only pension income after death but potentially other benefits that matter greatly to a surviving spouse.

That's why federal retirement planning deserves more than simply calculating the monthly annuity.

It requires understanding how the entire federal benefit package works together.

Specialized Federal Benefits Knowledge

Just as specialized Social Security education can be valuable, professional education exists specifically around federal employee benefits.

One designation is the **Chartered Federal Employee Benefits Consultant (ChFEBC)**, which focuses on the complexities surrounding federal employee retirement and benefit programs.

Another credential encountered in this area is the **Federal Retirement Consultant (FRC)** designation.

A credential doesn't automatically make someone the right advisor.

But if you're a federal employee approaching retirement, asking a financial professional about their specific knowledge and training in federal benefits is entirely reasonable.

Ask questions such as:

"How much experience do you have working with FERS?"

"Do you understand the TSP?"

"How does my survivor election affect my spouse?"

"What happens to our health insurance after I retire?"

"How should my federal pension coordinate with Social Security?"

"How do my federal benefits fit into the rest of my financial plan?"

If someone is helping you make retirement decisions involving benefits you've spent an entire career earning, they should understand how those benefits actually work.

A Special Note for Federal Employees

If you are a federal employee, your retirement deserves more attention than I can responsibly give it in a few pages of a general retirement book.

FERS, CSRS, the Thrift Savings Plan, FEHB, FEGLI, survivor elections, Social Security, sick-leave credit, special retirement provisions, and retirement timing can interact in ways that materially affect both your retirement and your surviving spouse.

That is why I wrote a companion book specifically for federal employees: Purpose Driven Federal Retirement — How to Turn Your Federal Employee Benefits Into the Life You've Been Planning For.

The principles in this book still apply. Your pension, TSP, Social Security, taxes, healthcare, insurance, estate plan, family, and purpose all need to work together. The federal edition simply takes those principles and applies them directly to the federal benefits system.

If you are a federal employee, I encourage you to use that book alongside this one.

The Irreversible Decision

> **Seek Counsel Before the Door Closes**
> *Some retirement choices are difficult or impossible to reverse. Scripture repeatedly values wise counsel. Getting help before an irreversible election is not weakness; it is prudence.*
> ***Scripture anchor: Proverbs 15:22***

This is perhaps the most important warning in this chapter.

Many pension elections become irrevocable once payments begin.

You may not get a second chance.

You can't necessarily come back five years later and say:

"We've changed our minds. We'd like the survivor option."

That's why the analysis should happen **before** the pension begins.

Not after.

Take your time.

Read the plan documents.

Request illustrations of every available option.

Understand the survivor provisions.

Understand the healthcare implications.

Understand the tax consequences.

Then make the decision in the context of your entire retirement plan.

Mark and Lisa Make the Pension Decision

Let's return to Mark and Lisa.

Mark has a pension.

Suppose he's given a choice between:

A larger single-life pension.

Or a smaller pension that continues to Lisa if Mark dies first.

At first, Mark likes the larger check.

Who wouldn't?

But then they revisit the survivor analysis from Chapter 5.

Mark has the larger Social Security benefit.

Lisa's Social Security benefit is smaller.

They've already considered delaying Mark's Social Security partly because it may strengthen Lisa's future survivor income.

Now they look at the pension.

If Mark takes the single-life pension and dies first:

One Social Security check disappears.

The pension disappears.

Lisa is left relying more heavily on the portfolio.

If Mark elects an appropriate survivor option:

One Social Security benefit still disappears.

But Lisa may retain Mark's larger Social Security benefit under the applicable survivor rules.

And part or all of the pension may continue.

Now her income floor is much stronger.

Does that automatically mean they should choose the survivor pension?

No.

But now they're evaluating the right problem.

They're no longer asking:

"How do we maximize Mark's pension?"

They're asking:

"How do we maximize the probability that both Mark and Lisa remain financially independent for the rest of their lives?"

That's the question that matters.

Your Purpose Driven Action Step

If you have a pension, gather your plan information and answer these questions.

1. What pension options are available?

Single life?

50% survivor?

75% survivor?

100% survivor?

Other options?

2. What is the monthly payment under each option?

Write them down side by side.

3. Does the pension include a cost-of-living adjustment?

If so, how does it work?

4. What happens when I die?

Be specific.

5. What happens if my spouse dies first?

Does the pension change?

6. What happens to retiree healthcare after either spouse dies?

7. Is there a lump-sum option?

If so, what are the advantages and risks?

8. How does the pension coordinate with Social Security?

9. What percentage of our essential expenses would remain covered after the first death?

10. Is the election permanent?

Don't sign the form until you understand the answer to every question.

Don't Maximize the Check. Maximize the Plan.

There is a theme developing.

With Social Security, the biggest immediate check isn't always the best decision.

With pensions, the biggest immediate check isn't always the best decision.

Later, we'll discover that the investment with the highest return isn't always the best investment.

The strategy that produces the smallest tax bill this year isn't always the best tax strategy.

And the estate plan that leaves the largest inheritance isn't necessarily the one that best reflects your values.

Retirement planning requires us to stop maximizing individual pieces.

Instead, we optimize the **whole**.

That's the difference between collecting financial products and building a financial plan.

Your pension has a job.

Your Social Security has a job.

Your investments have a job.

Your insurance has a job.

And each one should support the same purpose:

Creating the strongest possible retirement for you and the people you love.

We've now begun building the dependable portion of the retirement paycheck.

Social Security.

Pensions.

Other predictable income.

But for most retirees, those sources won't cover everything.

The rest must come from the assets they've spent decades accumulating.

And that creates a new question.

If your investment portfolio needs to provide income for the next twenty, thirty, or even forty years:

How should that money actually be invested?

That's where we're going next.

Part III — Managing the Money for a Lifetime

◆

Chapter 7

Investing After the Paycheck Stops

> **What Is Enough?**
> *Investing should serve a purpose beyond accumulation. Once the plan can reasonably provide, protect, and fund the life you value, the question becomes what additional wealth is meant to accomplish.*
> ***Scripture anchor: Luke 12:16–21***

Investing while you're working and investing after you retire are not the same thing.

Before retirement, market declines can be unpleasant.

After retirement, they can become personal.

When you're still earning a paycheck, you may actually benefit from market downturns because you're continuing to buy investments at lower prices.

You have income coming in.

You have time.

You may have decades before you need the money.

But once the paycheck stops, the rules change.

Now your portfolio may need to provide:

Monthly income.

Emergency reserves.

Future growth.

Inflation protection.

Healthcare funding.

Travel.

Family gifts.

And possibly an inheritance.

That is a much harder job.

The retirement portfolio doesn't just need to grow.

It needs to **work**.

Two Opposite Mistakes

Retirees often make one of two mistakes.

The first is staying too aggressive.

They remain invested as though they're still forty years old and accumulating assets.

Maybe they enjoyed strong investment returns before retirement.

Maybe they're afraid that becoming more conservative will mean missing out.

Maybe they believe they need 8%, 10%, or even 12% returns for the plan to work.

So they take more risk than the retirement plan can comfortably support.

Then the market falls.

Now they're withdrawing money from a declining portfolio.

That's where trouble can begin.

The second mistake is the opposite.

A retiree says:

"I can't afford to lose anything."

So they move almost everything to:

Cash.

CDs.

Money-market accounts.

Short-term fixed-income investments.

The account feels safe.

But now another risk begins growing quietly in the background.

Inflation.

If retirement lasts thirty years, being too conservative can be just as dangerous as being too aggressive.

The objective isn't:

Maximum return.

And it isn't:

No volatility.

The objective is:

The right amount of risk for the job your money needs to do.

Risk Tolerance Isn't Enough

Financial questionnaires often ask questions such as:

"How would you feel if your portfolio declined 20%?"

Would you:

Sell everything?

Sell some?

Do nothing?

Buy more?

These questions are trying to measure your **risk tolerance**.

That's useful.

But it isn't enough.

Retirement planning also requires us to understand your **risk capacity**.

The difference is important.

Risk tolerance asks:

"How much volatility can I emotionally tolerate?"

Risk capacity asks:

"How much loss can my financial plan actually afford?"

Those aren't always the same thing.

The Investor Who Loves Risk

Imagine someone who says:

"I've been investing for thirty years. Market declines don't bother me."

Wonderful.

Maybe this person truly has a high risk tolerance.

But suppose they retire with $1 million and need $70,000 per year from the portfolio to support basic expenses.

A major portfolio decline could significantly affect the sustainability of those withdrawals.

Emotionally, this person may be comfortable with risk.

Financially, they may have less capacity for it than they realize.

Now imagine someone else with $5 million invested, modest spending needs, substantial Social Security income, and a pension covering all essential expenses.

This person may have considerably more financial capacity for investment risk—even if they emotionally dislike volatility.

That's why we have to understand both.

Risk Required

There's actually a third concept.

Risk required.

How much investment risk does your financial plan actually require you to take to accomplish your goals?

This question can be surprisingly liberating.

Suppose someone has accumulated far more money than they reasonably need.

They have strong Social Security income.

A pension.

Little debt.

And their retirement plan works even with relatively modest investment returns.

Why take enormous risk?

They may have the ability to take more risk.

But they may not need to.

On the other hand, someone whose plan requires unrealistic returns simply to avoid running out of money doesn't necessarily have an investment problem.

They may have a planning problem.

The solution might involve:

Working longer.

Saving more.

Spending less.

Changing Social Security timing.

Reducing taxes.

Adjusting goals.

Or some combination.

Investment risk should not be used to rescue an otherwise unsustainable retirement plan.

Give Every Dollar a Time Horizon

One of the easiest ways to think about retirement investments is to stop viewing the portfolio as one giant pile of money.

Instead, ask:

When might I need these dollars?

Money needed next year has a very different job than money intended for twenty years from now.

Think about three broad time horizons.

Money for Today

These are dollars needed relatively soon.

Monthly withdrawals.

Emergency expenses.

Known major purchases.

This money needs liquidity.

Its primary purpose is not maximum growth.

Its purpose is availability.

Money for Tomorrow

These are assets that may fund spending several years from now.

They need some growth.

But they may also require greater stability than money with a very long time horizon.

Money for Much Later

These dollars may not be needed for ten, fifteen, or twenty years.

They have a very different job.

This portion may need to provide long-term growth and help protect against inflation.

The further away the goal, the more time investments generally have to recover from short-term market volatility.

This is why **time horizon and purpose should influence investment risk.**

Your Portfolio Doesn't Know You're Retired

The stock market doesn't care that you retired last Tuesday.

It doesn't know you need money next month.

It doesn't know that you're planning a vacation.

It doesn't know that your daughter is getting married.

The market will do what markets do.

Sometimes it will rise.

Sometimes it will fall.

And occasionally it will fall at exactly the wrong time.

That's why we don't build retirement income around the assumption that the market will cooperate with our calendar.

We build flexibility.

What Will You Sell During the Next Bear Market?

> **Prepare Before Fear Arrives**
> *The best time to decide how you will respond to a market decline is before the decline begins. Planning in calm conditions reduces the chance that fear will make the decision later.*
> ***Scripture anchor: Proverbs 22:3***

Here's a question every retiree should answer before investing the portfolio.

If the stock market falls 35% next year, where will my paycheck come from?

If the answer is:

"I guess I'll sell stocks."

We may have a problem.

What other assets are available?

Cash?

Short-term bonds?

Pension income?

Social Security?

A spending reserve?

Could some discretionary expenses be reduced?

The objective isn't to predict when the next bear market will occur.

It's to make sure the bear market doesn't control your retirement decisions when it does.

Beware of "Safe"

Investors often use the word *safe* without defining it.

Cash is safe from stock-market volatility.

But it isn't necessarily safe from inflation.

Long-term bonds may produce dependable income.

But their market values can still fluctuate, especially when interest rates change.

Stocks may be volatile over short periods.

But historically, diversified equity ownership has been an important source of long-term growth.

Different investments carry different risks.

So when someone says:

"I want a safe portfolio,"

my next question is:

"Safe from what?"

Market losses?

Inflation?

Running out of money?

Income interruption?

Interest-rate changes?

Credit risk?

Taxes?

There is no investment that protects perfectly against everything.

Diversification Isn't Owning a Lot of Things

People sometimes believe they are diversified because they own twelve mutual funds.

Maybe they are.

Maybe they aren't.

If all twelve funds own essentially the same types of companies, the portfolio may not be nearly as diversified as it appears.

Diversification means spreading exposure across different sources of investment risk.

That may include different:

Asset classes.

Company sizes.

Industries.

Geographies.

Investment styles.

Bond types.

Maturities.

And potentially other categories depending on the investor.

The goal is not to own everything.

It's to avoid allowing one particular risk to determine the outcome of your entire retirement.

Don't Confuse Diversification With Complexity

More investments do not automatically create a better portfolio.

I've seen portfolios containing dozens of funds.

Five different investment accounts.

Several annuities.

Individual stocks.

Multiple bond funds.

Structured products.

Old employer plans.

And nobody—including the owner—can explain why half of them are there.

Complexity can create the illusion of sophistication.

But a good retirement portfolio should be explainable.

You should understand:

What you own.

Why you own it.

What job it performs.

What risks it carries.

When you might use it.

If nobody can explain an investment in plain English, that's worth paying attention to.

Return Is Only Half the Conversation

Investors love talking about performance.

"What did I make last year?"

"How did I do compared with the S&P 500?"

Those can be reasonable questions.

But retirement planning requires additional questions.

How much risk did we take to achieve that return?

How much income did the portfolio need to generate?

How much volatility can the plan withstand?

What is the tax impact?

Did the portfolio accomplish its assigned job?

Suppose your neighbor earned 18% last year and you earned 12%.

Did your neighbor do better?

Maybe.

But what if their portfolio took twice as much risk?

What if they don't need their money for twenty years while you're already retired and withdrawing from yours?

The comparison may be meaningless.

Your benchmark isn't your neighbor.

Your benchmark is your plan.

The Danger of Chasing Yesterday's Winner

Every investment cycle creates stars.

Technology stocks.

Energy.

Real estate.

Gold.

Emerging markets.

Cryptocurrency.

Small companies.

Large companies.

Whatever performed best recently begins attracting attention.

Financial television talks about it.

Friends talk about it.

Articles appear.

Eventually investors start thinking:

"Why don't I own more of that?"

This can lead to one of the oldest investment mistakes:

Buying yesterday's winner.

The problem is that investment leadership changes.

What performed best last year may not perform best next year.

Retirement portfolios shouldn't be designed around guessing the next winner.

They should be designed around accomplishing the plan.

What About Individual Stocks?

Some retirees enjoy owning individual companies.

Maybe they've accumulated company stock over a career.

Maybe they simply enjoy investing.

That's fine.

But concentration risk deserves attention.

Suppose 40% of your retirement wealth is invested in a single company.

Perhaps it's the company you worked for.

You know the business.

You believe in management.

You feel connected to it.

But your retirement now depends heavily on the financial future of one organization.

The company may perform beautifully.

Or something unexpected may happen.

Industries change.

Competitors emerge.

Regulations change.

Management makes mistakes.

Technology changes.

Companies that once appeared invincible sometimes aren't.

Retirement planning requires asking whether the concentration risk is necessary.

Bonds Have Risk Too

When people retire, they often increase bond exposure.

That can make sense.

Bonds may help provide income and reduce overall portfolio volatility.

But "bond" does not mean "risk-free."

Bonds can carry:

Interest-rate risk.

Credit risk.

Inflation risk.

Liquidity risk.

Reinvestment risk.

Longer-term bonds may behave very differently from shorter-term bonds.

High-yield bonds may behave differently from high-quality government securities.

Once again:

Understand the job.

Understand the risk.

The Role of Growth

Now let's talk about something retirees sometimes try to eliminate.

Growth.

Suppose you retire at 65 and live to 95.

That's thirty years.

If your retirement plan becomes dramatically conservative on day one, how will your income keep pace with rising costs over three decades?

How will you fund healthcare later?

How will your portfolio support a surviving spouse who may live another ten years after you're gone?

That's why stocks and other growth-oriented assets don't necessarily disappear when retirement begins.

Their role changes.

We're no longer simply maximizing accumulation.

We're using growth strategically to support a long retirement.

The Role of Stability

At the same time, growth doesn't pay next month's bills reliably.

That's why we need stability too.

Stable assets can provide:

Liquidity.

Short-term income.

A source of withdrawals during market downturns.

Psychological comfort.

The ability to avoid selling long-term investments at the wrong time.

The tension between stability and growth isn't a problem to eliminate.

It's something to manage.

We need both.

The Portfolio Has Multiple Jobs

Remember the concept from Chapter 4?

Every dollar needs a job.

Let's apply that directly to investments.

Some assets may be assigned to:

Today's lifestyle

Some to:

Near-term income

Some to:

Emergencies

Some to:

Long-term growth

Some to:

Healthcare

Some to:

Legacy

Some to:

Charitable giving

Now investment decisions become much more purposeful.

Instead of saying:

"I think stocks are going down."

We're asking:

"What job is this money performing, and what investment strategy best supports that job?"

That's a much more disciplined approach.

Mark and Lisa Build Their Portfolio Around the Plan

Let's return to Mark and Lisa.

They have approximately $1.6 million in retirement and investment assets.

They've already identified:

Their essential expenses.

Their lifestyle expenses.

Social Security.

Mark's pension.

Their survivor-income needs.

Now we can begin designing the portfolio.

They know they'll need some portfolio withdrawals immediately after retirement.

Those dollars deserve liquidity.

They know they'll have several major travel expenses during the first few years.

Those dollars probably shouldn't depend entirely on short-term stock-market performance.

They also know Lisa could still be alive thirty or forty years from now.

That money needs long-term growth.

Suddenly, the portfolio isn't simply:

60% stocks.

40% bonds.

It's a collection of resources with different purposes and time horizons.

The allocation should reflect those jobs.

Don't Start With the Pie Chart

This may sound strange coming from someone discussing investments.

But don't begin your retirement plan with an asset-allocation pie chart.

Begin with your life.

How much income do you need?

What income is dependable?

What expenses are flexible?

What major purchases are coming?

What risks are we protecting against?

What is the time horizon?

What legacy goals exist?

Then we decide how the assets should be positioned.

The investment portfolio serves the plan.

The plan does not serve the portfolio.

Your Investment Stress Test

Let's test your current portfolio.

Ask yourself:

1. If the stock market falls 30% tomorrow, what happens to my retirement income?

2. How much money will I likely need from investments during the next three years?

3. Is that money exposed to more risk than necessary?

4. How much of my portfolio needs to grow for ten years or more?

5. Am I holding so much cash that inflation could threaten my long-term purchasing power?

6. Am I overly concentrated in one company, sector, or investment type?

7. Do I understand what every major investment in my portfolio is supposed to accomplish?

8. Could I emotionally tolerate the decline my current portfolio might experience?

9. More importantly, could my financial plan tolerate it?

10. What would I sell during the next major market downturn?

If you can't answer the last question, that is worth fixing before the downturn occurs.

Write an Investment Policy for Yourself

Large institutions often use investment policy statements.

Individuals can benefit from the same idea.

It doesn't need to be complicated.

Write down:

What your portfolio is designed to accomplish.

How much risk you're willing and able to take.

How much liquidity you need.

What percentage ranges you'll generally maintain across major investment categories.

How often you'll rebalance.

What circumstances would cause you to change the strategy.

And perhaps most importantly:

What will not cause you to change the strategy.

A frightening headline?

Not necessarily.

An election?

Not automatically.

A market prediction on television?

Probably not.

Your neighbor making money on something you don't own?

Definitely not.

A written investment philosophy can help protect you from making emotional decisions during emotional markets.

Rebalancing: Buying Low Without Predicting the Future

Suppose your desired portfolio includes both growth and defensive assets.

Stocks perform extremely well.

Eventually they represent a larger percentage of your portfolio than intended.

Rebalancing may involve selling some of what appreciated and adding to areas that now represent less than their target.

During a major decline, the opposite may occur.

Rebalancing is a disciplined process.

It doesn't require predicting what happens next.

You're simply restoring the portfolio to the risk profile the plan was designed around.

That's a very different behavior from chasing whatever recently performed best.

Stop Asking, "What Will the Market Do?"

One of the most common questions investors ask is:

"What do you think the market is going to do?"

Here's the frustrating answer.

Nobody knows consistently.

We can discuss valuations.

Interest rates.

Economic conditions.

Corporate earnings.

Historical patterns.

Politics.

Risks.

But none of those gives us reliable knowledge of what markets will do next week, next month, or next year.

A better retirement question is:

"What will we do if the market goes up?"

And:

"What will we do if it goes down?"

Now we have a strategy regardless of what happens.

Your Investment Strategy Should Help You Sleep

There's a financial answer to how much risk you should take.

And there's a human answer.

Both matter.

If your portfolio is so aggressive that you can't sleep during market declines, you may eventually make a terrible decision at exactly the wrong time.

If it's so conservative that you're constantly worried about running out of money twenty years from now, that's not comfortable either.

The right portfolio should create enough growth to support the plan while containing enough stability that you can remain disciplined.

That balance will be different for every person.

Never Take Risk Without a Reason

This is a principle worth remembering.

Every investment risk should have a reason.

Why are you owning stocks?

Long-term growth.

Why hold bonds?

Income and stability.

Why maintain cash?

Liquidity.

Why own a particular investment?

It should have an answer.

If the only explanation is:

"Because I think it's going up,"

that's speculation.

A retirement portfolio should be more intentional than that.

The Goal Is Not to Beat the Market

You might outperform the S&P 500.

You might underperform it.

But if you:

Fund your lifestyle.

Travel.

Help your family.

Maintain your independence.

Protect your spouse.

Stay ahead of inflation.

And never run out of money,

does it really matter whether your portfolio beat an index by 1.2%?

This is one of the strange things about investing.

People can become so focused on winning the investment competition that they forget what the money is for.

The market is not your goal.

Your life is.

Purpose Before Performance

> **Returns Serve the Plan**
> *Investment performance matters, but it is not the ultimate scorecard. A portfolio that supports income, family, giving, resilience, and the life you intend to live may be doing its job even when another investment temporarily earns more.*
> ***Scripture anchor: Luke 12:15***

Let's return to the idea that started this book.

What matters most?

If your investment strategy is disconnected from that answer, we're missing something.

Maybe your portfolio needs to fund twenty years of travel.

Maybe it needs to protect your spouse.

Maybe you want to leave money to grandchildren.

Maybe charitable giving is important.

Maybe your biggest priority is never having to ask your children for money.

Those goals determine what your investments need to accomplish.

Performance matters.

Risk matters.

Fees matter.

Taxes matter.

But none of them exists in isolation.

The portfolio's job is to support your Purpose Driven Retirement.

And that leads naturally to another major question.

Two portfolios can earn identical investment returns and still produce dramatically different retirement outcomes.

Why?

Because what you keep matters just as much as what you earn.

Taxes can affect:

Investment withdrawals.

Social Security.

Medicare premiums.

Required distributions.

Estate planning.

And the amount eventually inherited by your family.

Which means the next major risk we need to manage isn't in the stock market.

It's the tax code.

Chapter 8

Retirement Tax Planning — Stop Thinking One Year at a Time

> **Render to Caesar—And Remember the Rest**
> *Jesus' response about Caesar recognizes legitimate civic obligations while drawing a boundary around ultimate allegiance. Pay what is lawfully owed, use legitimate planning strategies, and do not make either taxation or tax avoidance the center of the plan.*
> ***Scripture anchor: Matthew 22:15–22***

Most people think about taxes once a year.

They gather their tax documents.

They send everything to their accountant.

They wait.

Then they find out whether they're getting a refund or writing a check.

That's tax preparation.

It's important.

But it isn't the same thing as tax planning.

Tax preparation looks backward.

It asks:

"What happened last year, and how much do I owe?"

Tax planning looks forward.

It asks:

"What decisions can we make now that may improve our tax situation over the next ten, twenty, or thirty years?"

That distinction becomes incredibly important in retirement.

Because retirement may give you more control over your taxable income than you've had during most of your working life.

And if you don't use that control intentionally, you may miss opportunities that never come back.

Your Tax Return Is Not Your Tax Plan

Imagine someone retires at 65.

Their accountant prepares an excellent tax return every year.

Every deduction is claimed.

Every form is correct.

Every deadline is met.

That's great.

But suppose this retiree also has $2 million in traditional retirement accounts.

They take only what they need each year.

The accounts continue growing.

Eventually required minimum distributions begin.

Now large amounts are being forced out of those accounts.

Taxable income rises.

Medicare premiums may rise.

Social Security taxation may increase.

Then one spouse dies.

The survivor is eventually filing as a single taxpayer while still owning much of the same retirement wealth.

Suddenly, the tax problem becomes even larger.

The tax returns may have been prepared perfectly every year.

But was there a tax strategy?

Those are two different things.

The Goal Isn't Zero Taxes

> **Render to Caesar**
> *When Jesus was challenged about taxes, He rejected both tax rebellion and government worship: give Caesar what belongs to Caesar, and give God what belongs to God. For retirement planning, that suggests a balanced principle: pay legitimate obligations, use lawful strategies to avoid needless tax, and never allow tax minimization to become the purpose of the plan.*
> ***Scripture anchor: Matthew 22:15-22***

Let's get something out of the way.

You probably aren't going to retire and legally pay zero taxes for the rest of your life.

And that shouldn't necessarily be the objective.

The goal is generally to pay the **appropriate amount of tax at the most advantageous times available to you**.

Sometimes that may mean reducing income.

Sometimes it may actually mean intentionally creating taxable income today.

That sounds backward.

Why would anyone voluntarily pay tax sooner?

Because sometimes paying tax at a lower rate today can reduce the amount exposed to a potentially higher rate later.

This is where retirement tax planning gets interesting.

Meet the Tax Mountain

Imagine your taxable income over your lifetime as a landscape.

During your working years, income may be relatively high.

Then you retire.

Suddenly your salary disappears.

You may have several years where taxable income drops.

Later:

Social Security begins.

Pensions begin.

Required distributions begin.

Perhaps one spouse dies.

Your income may rise again or your tax filing situation may become less favorable.

That creates something we might call a **tax valley**.

And those lower-income years can create opportunities.

The Retirement Tax Valley

Suppose you retire at 63.

Your salary stops.

You haven't started Social Security yet.

Required minimum distributions are still years away.

You have money available from:

Cash.

Taxable investments.

Roth accounts.

Perhaps part-time work.

Your taxable income could be considerably lower than it was while you were working.

That's not simply a nice tax year.

It may be a planning opportunity.

Maybe you intentionally withdraw additional money from a traditional IRA.

Maybe you convert some traditional IRA assets to a Roth IRA.

You pay tax now.

Why?

Because those dollars may otherwise remain tax-deferred, continue growing, and eventually become taxable later when your income or tax rates may be higher.

We're not trying to minimize this year's tax bill.

We're trying to manage the **lifetime tax bill**.

Roth Conversions: Paying Tax on Purpose

A Roth conversion is one of the clearest examples of purposeful tax planning.

In simplified terms, money moves from a traditional retirement account into a Roth account.

The converted amount generally becomes taxable income in the year of conversion.

That sounds unpleasant.

And it can be.

But consider the trade.

You're voluntarily paying tax today in exchange for moving money into an account that may provide qualified tax-free withdrawals later.

That can potentially create several benefits.

Future taxable required distributions may be reduced.

You may have greater flexibility in retirement.

Your surviving spouse may inherit a different tax structure.

Your beneficiaries may receive assets with different tax characteristics.

But Roth conversions are not automatically good.

The amount matters.

The timing matters.

The tax bracket matters.

Medicare matters.

Cash flow matters.

Estate goals matter.

This is strategy, not a slogan.

Don't Let the Tax Tail Wag the Dog

People sometimes become so obsessed with avoiding tax that they make financially poor decisions.

For example:

"I can't sell that investment because I'll owe capital-gains tax."

Maybe.

But what if the investment now represents 50% of your portfolio?

Avoiding a tax bill may be exposing your retirement to excessive concentration risk.

Or:

"I'll never withdraw from my IRA because I don't want taxable income."

But perhaps today's tax bracket is relatively attractive compared with the bracket you may face later.

Tax consequences matter.

But taxes are one part of the plan.

Never make a bad financial decision solely to avoid paying a tax.

The objective is to improve the entire financial outcome.

Your Traditional IRA Has a Silent Partner

Let's say you have $1 million in a traditional IRA.

It's easy to think:

"I have a million dollars."

Economically, that's not exactly true.

Some portion of that account may eventually belong to the government in the form of taxes.

We don't necessarily know how much.

It depends on:

Your future withdrawals.

Your tax rate.

Future tax law.

Your filing status.

Your state.

And other factors.

That's one reason I don't view all retirement dollars as identical.

A million dollars in a traditional IRA is different from a million dollars in a Roth IRA.

And both are different from a million dollars in a taxable investment account.

The account type matters because the tax treatment matters.

Tax Diversification

You've probably heard of investment diversification.

Don't put everything into one stock.

Don't put everything into one asset class.

There's another type of diversification worth considering:

Tax diversification.

If every dollar you own is in a traditional retirement account, you have relatively little flexibility.

Every dollar you withdraw may create taxable income.

But suppose you also have:

Roth assets.

Taxable investments.

Cash.

Now you may have choices.

Need $50,000 for a car?

You may be able to decide which source produces the most favorable overall result.

Need more spending money one year?

You may have multiple options.

Want to manage taxable income near a Medicare threshold?

Account flexibility may help.

Tax diversification gives you more levers to pull.

Required Minimum Distributions

Eventually, the government generally requires distributions from many tax-deferred retirement accounts.

These are commonly known as **required minimum distributions**, or RMDs.

The rules surrounding the applicable starting age and account types can change over time, so retirees should verify the current rules when approaching retirement.

The concept, however, is straightforward.

At some point, the government says:

"You've deferred taxes long enough. Start taking money out."

Whether you need the money or not.

That's where large traditional retirement balances can create tax problems.

The RMD Snowball

Imagine someone retires with $1.5 million in traditional retirement accounts.

They don't need much money from the accounts.

So they take very little.

The investments grow.

Years later the account is significantly larger.

Then required distributions begin under the rules applicable to the account owner. Under current federal law, the applicable RMD age is generally 73 for people born from 1951 through 1959 and 75 for people born in 1960 or later, with additional rules and exceptions for certain employer plans and owners.

Now sizable amounts must be withdrawn each year.

Those distributions may:

Increase taxable income.

Push part of income into higher tax brackets.

Increase the taxation of Social Security.

Affect Medicare premiums.

Increase the tax burden of a surviving spouse.

Potentially reduce future planning flexibility.

This is why "I'll leave the IRA alone as long as possible" isn't automatically the best strategy.

Sometimes intentionally reducing the tax-deferred balance earlier can improve the long-term plan.

Current-law note (2026): RMD rules are date-of-birth and account specific. Roth IRAs and designated Roth accounts in employer plans generally do not require lifetime RMDs for the original owner under current law. Always verify the rule that applies in the year a decision is made.

Bracket Management

One of the most powerful tax-planning ideas is surprisingly simple.

Don't just ask:

"What tax bracket am I in?"

Ask:

"How much room do I have left in that bracket?"

Suppose your taxable income places you comfortably inside a particular tax bracket.

You may be able to realize additional income while still staying within that marginal bracket.

That additional income might come from:

A Roth conversion.

An IRA withdrawal.

Capital gains.

Other sources.

The goal isn't necessarily to fill every tax bracket every year.

The point is that unused lower-tax opportunities may disappear later.

"But My Taxes Will Be Lower in Retirement"

This is one of the most common assumptions in financial planning.

Maybe.

But let's examine it.

During your working years, you have:

A salary.

Retirement-plan contributions.

Potential deductions.

Maybe children.

Perhaps a mortgage deduction.

Then you retire.

Your salary disappears.

It seems obvious taxes should fall.

But later retirement may include:

Social Security.

Pension income.

Required distributions.

Investment income.

Potentially fewer deductions.

Then one spouse dies and the survivor may eventually file as a single taxpayer.

Now the assumption that retirement automatically means low taxes looks less certain.

We don't know what future tax rates will be.

That's why diversification and planning matter.

The Widow or Widower Tax Problem

We briefly introduced this issue earlier.

Now let's look at it through the tax lens.

Suppose Mark and Lisa are married and retired.

They file jointly.

They own substantial retirement assets.

Then Mark dies.

What happens?

Eventually Lisa may file as a single taxpayer.

But she may still own:

The same house.

Most of the retirement accounts.

Much of the investment portfolio.

And she may receive Mark's larger Social Security benefit instead of her smaller one.

Many expenses remain.

But tax brackets and other thresholds may be less favorable for a single taxpayer than they were for a married couple filing jointly.

This is sometimes called the **widow's penalty** or **survivor tax penalty** in retirement planning.

It's not a specific IRS penalty.

It's the financial effect of changing from married filing jointly to single status while retaining significant taxable income.

Tax Planning Is Survivor Planning

Remember why Mark considered delaying his larger Social Security benefit?

To strengthen Lisa's survivor income.

Remember why they evaluated the joint-and-survivor pension?

To strengthen Lisa's future income floor.

Tax planning should follow the same logic.

If Mark and Lisa have a large traditional IRA, perhaps some strategic Roth conversions during their joint lifetimes could improve Lisa's future tax situation.

Again:

We're not just planning for Mark and Lisa today.

We're planning for:

Mark and Lisa.

Then Mark alone or Lisa alone.

Retirement planning needs to work through all three possibilities.

Social Security Taxation

Here's another area people often misunderstand.

Social Security isn't always tax-free.

Depending on your broader income picture, part of your Social Security benefits may be included in taxable income under federal rules.

That means a retirement-account withdrawal can sometimes affect more than just the tax on that withdrawal.

It can also affect how much Social Security becomes taxable.

This is sometimes referred to as part of the Social Security **tax torpedo** effect.

The technical calculations can be complicated.

The planning lesson is simple:

One additional dollar of income can sometimes affect more than one tax calculation.

Medicare IRMAA: The Tax That Isn't Called a Tax

Now we need to talk about Medicare.

Higher-income Medicare beneficiaries may pay additional premiums through what is known as the **Income-Related Monthly Adjustment Amount**, or IRMAA.

Technically, IRMAA isn't an income tax.

But from a retirement-planning standpoint, it can feel very similar.

Your income rises.

Your Medicare costs rise.

That means decisions involving taxable income may affect:

Federal income tax.

Social Security taxation.

And Medicare premiums.

That's why we shouldn't evaluate a Roth conversion by simply asking:

"What tax bracket does this put me in?"

We also need to ask:

"What else does the additional income affect?"

Beware the Two-Year Lookback

Medicare income-related premium adjustments generally use modified adjusted gross income from the tax return filed two years earlier, although more recent information may be used in certain circumstances.

That can surprise retirees.

You retire.

Your income drops.

Then you enroll in Medicare and discover that premiums are based on income from when you were still earning a large salary.

There are circumstances where certain life-changing events may allow an appeal or reconsideration under Social Security Administration rules.

Retirement itself can be one such qualifying event when the applicable requirements are met.

The important lesson is:

Don't assume the Medicare premium is permanent just because the first bill is high.

Understand the rules.

Charitable Giving Can Be Tax Planning Too

> **Impact First, Tax Benefit Second**
> *Tax efficiency can increase the resources available for generosity, but the deduction should not become the reason for the gift. Begin with whom or what you want to help; then structure the giving intelligently.*
> ***Scripture anchor: 2 Corinthians 9:7***

If charitable giving is important to you, the way you give can matter.

Writing a check is generous.

But there may be more tax-efficient ways to accomplish the same charitable goal.

For example, some people may benefit from giving appreciated securities instead of cash.

Others who meet applicable age and eligibility rules may use qualified charitable distributions from IRAs.

Donor-advised funds may be appropriate in certain situations.

There are many possibilities.

The point isn't to give money away simply to save taxes.

You never become wealthier by giving away a dollar solely to avoid paying a fraction of that dollar in tax.

But if you were already planning to give the money:

Why not give it intelligently?

Qualified Charitable Distributions

For charitably inclined IRA owners who meet applicable rules, a **Qualified Charitable Distribution**, often abbreviated QCD, may allow money to move directly from an IRA to an eligible charitable organization.

When properly structured, a QCD can be excluded from taxable income and can count toward an applicable IRA required minimum distribution. Under current federal rules, the IRA owner generally must be at least age 70½ when the distribution is made, and other eligibility, charity, annual-limit, and reporting requirements apply.

That can make QCDs an extremely useful retirement-planning tool for the right person.

But eligibility requirements, annual limits, qualified charities, and reporting rules matter.

Always verify current law before acting.

Roth Doesn't Always Mean Spend It Last

You've probably heard rules of thumb like:

"Spend taxable accounts first."

"Then traditional IRAs."

"Spend Roth accounts last."

That may sometimes make sense.

It is not a universal law.

Suppose taking additional traditional IRA money would create:

A higher marginal tax rate.

More Social Security taxation.

Higher Medicare premiums.

Maybe using some Roth money instead makes sense.

In another year, perhaps intentionally taking more traditional IRA money is exactly what the plan calls for.

Withdrawal strategy should be dynamic.

The Tax-Control Account

One way to think about Roth assets is as a **tax-control account**.

Suppose you need an additional $30,000 one year.

If the money comes from a traditional IRA, taxable income generally rises.

If it comes from a qualified Roth distribution, taxable income generally does not.

That gives you control.

Control can be incredibly valuable when managing:

Tax brackets.

Medicare premiums.

Capital gains.

Large purchases.

Survivor income.

The Roth account isn't simply "tax-free money."

It's a planning tool.

The Tax Opportunity Window

For many retirees, the most important tax-planning period may be the years immediately after retirement.

Salary has stopped.

Social Security may not have begun.

Required distributions haven't started.

Maybe there's a five-year window.

Maybe seven.

Maybe ten.

Those years can pass quickly.

Once they're gone, they're gone.

That's why tax planning should begin **before retirement**, not after RMDs become a problem.

Mark and Lisa Find Their Tax Window

Let's return to Mark and Lisa.

Mark retires at 65.

Lisa is slightly younger.

They have substantial traditional retirement assets.

Mark's pension begins.

They have taxable investments and cash available.

They are considering delaying Mark's larger Social Security benefit.

Suddenly, the years before both Social Security benefits and future required distributions are fully in place become interesting.

Their taxable income may be lower than it was during Mark's working years.

Could they convert some traditional IRA assets to Roth?

Maybe.

Should they convert the entire IRA immediately?

Probably not without a very good reason.

Instead, they might evaluate conversions annually.

How much room exists in their preferred tax bracket?

How does the conversion affect Medicare?

How much cash is available to pay tax?

How would future RMDs change?

What happens to Lisa's tax situation if Mark dies first?

Now tax planning is integrated with:

Social Security.

Pension planning.

Medicare.

Investment withdrawals.

Survivor planning.

Exactly as it should be.

Your Lifetime Tax Map

Here's an exercise worth doing.

Draw a horizontal timeline.

Start with your current age.

Then mark:

Retirement.

Social Security claiming dates.

Pension start dates.

Medicare eligibility.

Required distribution age under current law (generally age 73 or 75 depending on date of birth, subject to account type and other rules).

Major planned asset sales.

Possible inheritance events if reasonably foreseeable.

Then ask:

Where might taxable income be lowest?

Those are potential planning windows.

Now ask:

Where might taxable income rise sharply?

Those are potential tax-pressure points.

You're beginning to create a lifetime tax map.

Your Purpose Driven Action Step

Answer the following questions.

1. How much of our retirement money is tax-deferred?

2. How much is Roth?

3. How much is taxable?

4. What might our income look like immediately after retirement?

5. When will Social Security begin?

6. When will pension income begin?

7. When are required distributions expected to begin under current law?

8. Are there years where taxable income may temporarily be lower?

9. Would Roth conversions deserve consideration during those years?

10. How could additional income affect Medicare premiums?

11. What happens to the tax situation after the first spouse dies?

12. Are there charitable strategies that fit goals we already have?

13. Are we making tax decisions one year at a time—or over an entire lifetime?

That final question is the most important.

Tax Planning Is About Flexibility

Nobody knows exactly what future tax laws will be.

We don't know exactly what marginal tax rates will look like twenty years from now.

That's another reason not to build a retirement plan dependent on one tax outcome.

If you have:

Traditional money.

Roth money.

Taxable money.

Cash.

You may have options.

If future taxes rise, you have choices.

If future taxes fall, you have choices.

If Medicare thresholds become important, you have choices.

If a spouse dies, you have choices.

Financial flexibility creates tax flexibility.

Don't Wait Until December 31

Good tax planning often requires action before the year is over.

Sometimes well before.

Roth conversions.

Charitable distributions.

Capital gains.

Tax losses.

Retirement withdrawals.

Estimated tax payments.

Medicare planning.

These decisions may need coordination between your:

Financial advisor.

Tax professional.

Estate-planning attorney.

And sometimes other specialists.

The people helping you shouldn't operate in separate silos.

Your tax professional shouldn't discover your Roth conversion when the 1099 arrives.

Your financial advisor shouldn't learn about a major capital gain after the sale has already happened.

Planning works best when the professionals communicate before the decision is made.

The Goal Is After-Tax Retirement Income

Let's come back to where Part II began.

Your retirement paycheck.

Suppose two retirees each receive $120,000 per year.

One keeps $105,000 after taxes and related costs.

The other keeps $90,000.

Those retirees do not have the same retirement income.

That's why I care less about gross income than **spendable income**.

And that's why investment performance alone doesn't determine retirement success.

What matters is what ultimately reaches your life.

Your travel.

Your home.

Your grandchildren.

Your healthcare.

Your generosity.

Your financial independence.

The IRS doesn't care what your retirement dreams are.

But your financial plan should.

Don't Ask Only, "How Much Tax Will I Pay?"

Ask:

When will I pay it?

At what rate?

From which account?

What other consequences does that income create?

What happens later?

What happens after one spouse dies?

What happens to the people who inherit what's left?

Now we're no longer preparing a tax return.

We're planning.

Purpose Before Taxes

Nobody's retirement goal is:

"I want to die having paid the lowest possible amount of income tax."

Your goal might be:

Traveling with your spouse.

Helping your children.

Leaving something to grandchildren.

Supporting your church.

Maintaining independence.

Enjoying your life.

Taxes simply influence how efficiently your resources can support those purposes.

So yes, we should manage them intelligently.

But the purpose remains larger than the tax strategy.

Keep more of what you've built—not simply so the number stays larger, but so more of your money can go toward the things you actually care about.

And taxes aren't the only expense that can change dramatically in retirement.

For many people, the next one is even more personal.

Healthcare.

Medicare.

Prescription drugs.

Long-term care.

And the question nobody really wants to ask:

"What happens if I need help taking care of myself?"

That's where we're going next.

Part IV — Protecting Your Independence

◆

Chapter 9

Healthcare and Medicare — The Expense You Can't Ignore

There are some retirement expenses people enjoy planning for.

Travel.

A second home.

Golf.

Hobbies.

Grandchildren.

Dining out.

Healthcare usually isn't one of them.

Nobody dreams about retirement by saying:

"I can't wait to spend more time thinking about insurance premiums, prescription coverage, deductibles, and Medicare."

But healthcare is one of those areas where ignoring the details can create very real financial problems.

And unlike a vacation or a new car, healthcare isn't always optional.

You may be able to postpone a trip.

You may be able to keep your current vehicle another year.

You probably cannot postpone a major medical need simply because it arrived during a bad market.

That's why healthcare deserves its own place in the retirement plan.

Retirement Healthcare Is More Than Medicare

Many people reach their early sixties believing that healthcare will become simple once Medicare begins.

Not exactly.

Medicare is enormously valuable.

But Medicare is not the same thing as free healthcare.

Depending on your situation, retirement healthcare costs can include:

Medicare premiums.

Supplemental insurance.

Medicare Advantage plan costs.

Prescription drug coverage.

Deductibles.

Copayments.

Coinsurance.

Dental care.

Vision care.

Hearing care.

Services not fully covered by Medicare.

Long-term care.

And out-of-pocket costs that may change from year to year.

So when someone tells me:

"We've budgeted $500 a month for healthcare,"

my next question is:

"What exactly does that include?"

That's where planning begins.

The Healthcare Bridge

One of the first healthcare problems retirees may face happens before Medicare even begins.

Suppose you want to retire at 62.

Financially, you can afford it.

You have investments.

Your retirement-income plan works.

Your Social Security strategy is in place.

Wonderful.

But you're several years away from Medicare eligibility.

Where does health insurance come from?

That can be one of the biggest obstacles to early retirement.

Possible solutions may include:

Employer retiree coverage.

Coverage through a spouse.

COBRA for a period of time.

Coverage purchased through the individual market.

Other employer or government programs depending on eligibility.

The right answer varies.

But the important point is this:

You don't have a complete retirement date until you have a healthcare bridge.

Don't Pick a Retirement Date Without Pricing Healthcare

This sounds simple, but it is often overlooked.

Someone says:

"I've decided I'm retiring next June."

Great.

How much will health insurance cost?

"I don't know yet."

That's backward.

Healthcare may materially affect the amount of income you need.

And if both spouses retire before Medicare eligibility, the cost may be significant.

That doesn't mean early retirement is impossible.

It means the expense needs to be included before you make the decision.

The retirement date should fit the entire plan.

Not just the investment portfolio.

Medicare Has Multiple Parts for a Reason

Medicare can feel confusing because it isn't one single insurance policy.

There are different parts and coverage structures.

At a high level, Medicare includes coverage associated with:

Hospital care.

Physician and outpatient services.

Prescription medications.

And private-plan alternatives or supplements depending on the structure selected.

You do not need to become a Medicare expert to retire successfully.

But you should understand enough to know that choosing coverage is not simply:

"I turned 65, so now I have Medicare."

There are decisions to make.

And the decisions should reflect your health, prescriptions, providers, travel habits, financial situation, and preferences.

Medicare Doesn't Cover Everything

This is one of the most important assumptions to correct.

Medicare can cover a substantial portion of healthcare expenses.

But it doesn't eliminate all healthcare costs.

And it generally isn't designed to pay indefinitely for custodial long-term care simply because someone needs assistance with everyday living.

That distinction matters enormously.

Medical care and long-term care are related.

They are not the same financial problem.

We'll devote the next chapter specifically to long-term care.

For now, understand that Medicare should be viewed as an important component of your retirement healthcare plan—not the entire plan.

Original Medicare Versus Medicare Advantage

Retirees commonly face a decision between different approaches to Medicare coverage.

One path may involve Original Medicare, often paired with separate prescription coverage and potentially supplemental insurance.

Another path may involve a Medicare Advantage plan provided through a private insurer.

Each structure has advantages and tradeoffs.

The right answer may depend on things such as:

Provider networks.

Prescription drugs.

Travel.

Premiums.

Out-of-pocket limits.

Specialist access.

Convenience.

Health conditions.

And personal preference.

This is not a decision that should be made based solely on which television commercial has the happiest retirees.

Read the details.

Understand the network.

Check your physicians.

Check your prescriptions.

Understand what happens if your health changes.

The Cheapest Premium May Not Be the Cheapest Plan

Here's a mistake consumers sometimes make.

They compare plans only by monthly premium.

Plan A costs less.

Plan B costs more.

Therefore Plan A must be better.

Maybe.

But insurance isn't purchased just to minimize premiums.

The real cost includes:

Premiums.

Deductibles.

Copays.

Coinsurance.

Prescription costs.

Out-of-network expenses.

Potential maximum out-of-pocket exposure.

And the financial impact of the services you actually use.

A plan with a lower premium can sometimes result in higher total costs depending on your healthcare needs.

This principle applies well beyond Medicare.

Price the risk, not just the premium.

Medicare and Income

Now let's connect healthcare back to taxes.

Higher-income Medicare beneficiaries may pay additional income-related premiums under the Medicare system.

We introduced this in Chapter 8 when discussing IRMAA.

Why does this matter?

Because your retirement income decisions can affect healthcare costs.

A large IRA withdrawal.

A Roth conversion.

A capital gain.

The sale of a business.

A major bonus before retirement.

Other taxable income.

These events may influence Medicare premiums depending on the applicable rules and measurement period.

Suddenly, a tax decision is also a healthcare decision.

Once again:

Everything connects.

The Two-Year Surprise

Medicare income-related adjustments often use tax information from an earlier year.

This can surprise someone who has just retired.

Imagine:

You earned a high salary.

Then you retire.

Your current income is much lower.

But Medicare premium calculations initially reflect an earlier tax year when your income was considerably higher.

You may look at the premium and think:

"This doesn't make any sense. I don't earn that anymore."

In certain situations involving qualifying life-changing events, there may be procedures to request reconsideration using more current income information.

Retirement can be relevant in that process when the requirements are met.

The important lesson is not to assume the first premium determination is always the final answer.

Understand the rules.

A Healthcare Reserve

Some retirees may find it useful to mentally or financially designate part of their resources specifically for future healthcare expenses.

That doesn't necessarily require opening a special account.

It means recognizing:

This portion of our wealth exists partly to protect our independence later.

Maybe that reserve stays invested differently because the need may be years away.

Maybe some of it is kept liquid.

Maybe insurance covers part of the risk.

The exact structure varies.

But giving healthcare dollars a job can help prevent the false belief that every retirement dollar is available for immediate lifestyle spending.

Health Savings Accounts

For people who accumulated money in a Health Savings Account, or HSA, during their working years, those assets may become particularly valuable in retirement.

HSAs can have attractive tax characteristics when used according to applicable rules for qualified medical expenses.

For some retirees, an HSA effectively becomes a dedicated healthcare resource.

That can make it an important part of the broader retirement strategy.

But again, don't view the account in isolation.

Ask:

When should we use it?

What expenses qualify?

Should we preserve some of it for later healthcare needs?

How does it fit with our other retirement accounts?

The account's value comes from how intentionally it is used.

The Health Expense Nobody Budgets For

There is another healthcare cost that doesn't always show up on financial projections.

Convenience.

As people age, they may begin paying for things they previously did themselves.

Lawn care.

Housekeeping.

Transportation.

Meal delivery.

Home maintenance.

Personal assistance.

These aren't technically medical expenses.

But they can become part of the financial cost of aging.

Someone may remain completely independent while still spending substantially more to maintain that independence.

That's worth planning for.

Independence Has a Price Tag

Think about what financial independence means at age 65.

Maybe it means:

Travel whenever you want.

Live wherever you want.

Spend without asking anyone for help.

At age 85, financial independence may mean something different.

It may mean:

Remaining in your own home.

Paying someone to drive you.

Hiring help with household tasks.

Affording the healthcare providers you prefer.

Moving into a community that offers more support.

Avoiding financial dependence on your children.

That's still financial independence.

The definition simply changed.

This is why healthcare and aging aren't side issues.

They connect directly to the purpose of retirement planning.

Couples Should Plan for Different Health Outcomes

A married couple may begin retirement together.

But they may not age the same way.

One spouse may remain healthy and active into their nineties.

The other may develop significant medical needs much earlier.

That can create financial and emotional pressure.

Ask:

What if one spouse needs substantially more healthcare than the other?

What if one spouse becomes the caregiver?

What happens to travel plans?

What happens to household income?

What happens if the caregiver can no longer provide care?

Those are difficult questions.

But answering them early can reduce stress later.

The Caregiver Risk

When people think about healthcare costs, they often think only about the person receiving care.

But illness can affect the healthy spouse financially too.

Suppose one spouse becomes seriously ill.

The other may:

Reduce work.

Stop working.

Travel frequently for treatment.

Modify the home.

Hire assistance.

Take over financial responsibilities.

Experience significant emotional stress.

The financial impact is often larger than a single hospital bill.

The entire household can change.

That's why good healthcare planning considers both spouses.

Mark and Lisa Plan for Healthcare

Let's return to Mark and Lisa.

They're approaching retirement.

Mark will be eligible for Medicare before Lisa.

That creates a temporary coverage gap for Lisa.

So their retirement plan has to account for:

Mark's Medicare premiums and coverage.

Lisa's temporary pre-Medicare insurance.

Prescription costs.

Supplemental coverage decisions.

Future Medicare premiums for both spouses.

Potential income-related premium adjustments.

Out-of-pocket medical expenses.

Long-term care risk.

Now imagine Mark simply looked at their investment plan and said:

"We have $1.6 million. We're ready."

Maybe.

But without healthcare included, we don't actually know.

Once the healthcare costs are built into their cash flow, the plan becomes much more realistic.

Federal Employees and Healthcare

Federal employees may have an especially important retirement healthcare consideration.

For eligible federal retirees who meet the applicable requirements, continuation of Federal Employees Health Benefits coverage into retirement can be extremely valuable.

But eligibility rules matter.

Retirement timing matters.

Enrollment history matters.

Survivor considerations matter.

Coordination with Medicare matters.

This is another example of why federal retirement benefits should be evaluated as a system.

FERS.

TSP.

Social Security.

FEHB.

Survivor elections.

Medicare.

They all interact.

A federal employee should understand the healthcare consequences of retirement **before** signing retirement paperwork.

Not afterward.

Retiree Coverage Can Be Worth More Than It Looks

Whether you're a federal employee, public employee, union member, corporate retiree, or someone with another employer-sponsored retiree plan, healthcare benefits may have significant economic value.

When comparing:

Retiring now.

Working another year.

Taking a different job.

Accepting an early-retirement package.

Don't compare salary and pension alone.

Ask:

What happens to healthcare?

What will replacing that coverage cost?

Can my spouse remain covered?

What happens before Medicare?

What happens after Medicare?

Healthcare can materially change the value of a retirement offer.

Medicare Enrollment Mistakes Can Be Expensive

Medicare enrollment rules can depend on:

Age.

Current employment.

Employer coverage.

Spousal coverage.

The size and type of employer plan.

Other circumstances.

Missing an enrollment window can potentially create coverage problems or penalties under applicable rules.

This isn't an area where guessing is wise.

Before retiring around Medicare eligibility, confirm:

When should I enroll?

Which parts do I need?

Does my employer coverage allow me to delay certain enrollment?

Does my spouse's coverage affect me?

How does retiree coverage coordinate?

Get the answer before employer coverage ends.

Don't Assume Human Resources Is Your Financial Planner

Employer human-resources departments can be enormously helpful.

They know the employer plan.

But remember their role.

They may explain:

What benefits exist.

How to elect them.

What deadlines apply.

What forms are required.

They may not be responsible for determining how those benefits fit into:

Your investment strategy.

Your Social Security decision.

Your spouse's retirement.

Your taxes.

Your estate plan.

Your long-term care strategy.

You still need to connect the pieces.

Your Purpose Driven Action Step

Before retirement, answer the following questions.

1. Where will our health insurance come from between retirement and Medicare eligibility?

2. What will it realistically cost?

3. When should each spouse enroll in Medicare?

4. Which Medicare structure fits our needs?

5. Are our doctors and healthcare systems included?

6. How are our prescriptions covered?

7. What are our likely out-of-pocket costs?

8. Could our income increase Medicare premiums?

9. Are there income events we should coordinate with Medicare planning?

10. Do we have retiree health coverage available from an employer?

11. What happens to that coverage after the first spouse dies?

12. Do we have HSA assets or other money specifically available for healthcare?

13. Who would make medical decisions if we couldn't?

14. Who could manage our finances during a medical emergency?

15. What happens if healthcare costs are much higher than expected?

You don't need perfect answers.

You need a plan.

Budget for Health, Plan for Independence

Healthcare planning isn't about predicting every illness.

You can't.

It's about recognizing that health affects nearly every part of retirement.

Income.

Spending.

Housing.

Travel.

Taxes.

Insurance.

Family.

Estate planning.

And independence.

When we prepare for healthcare expenses, we're not simply protecting money.

We're protecting your ability to make choices.

Where you live.

Who provides your care.

Which doctors you see.

Whether your spouse remains financially secure.

Whether your children have to step in.

Those choices matter.

The Question Behind the Healthcare Plan

Remember the central question of this book:

What matters most?

For many people, one answer appears again and again.

"I don't want to be a burden on my children."

That statement has enormous financial meaning.

It means healthcare matters.

Legal documents matter.

Cash reserves matter.

Insurance matters.

Long-term care matters.

Your housing plan matters.

And your family needs to understand your wishes before a crisis occurs.

That's why our next chapter goes beyond Medicare.

Because eventually healthcare may not be about visiting a doctor or filling a prescription.

It may be about needing help with everyday life.

Bathing.

Dressing.

Eating.

Transportation.

Medication management.

Remaining safely in your home.

Or moving somewhere that can provide additional support.

This is where many families find themselves making enormous financial decisions during one of the most emotional periods of their lives.

We can do better than that.

We can have the conversation before the crisis.

And it begins with a question most of us would rather avoid:

"If I need long-term care someday, what do I want that care to look like—and how will we pay for it?"

Choose Coverage Around Your Life

Premiums matter, but so do your doctors, hospitals, prescriptions, travel habits, and tolerance for out-of-pocket costs. A plan that works beautifully for your neighbor may be a poor fit for you.

The point is not to find the plan with the smallest number on the premium line. It is to choose coverage that supports the way you actually expect to live in retirement.

Chapter 10

Long-Term Care

Protecting Dignity, Independence, and Family

Long-term care is one of those topics most people would rather avoid.

It is understandable.

Nobody wants to imagine needing help with bathing, dressing, eating, using the bathroom, moving around, managing medications, or simply getting through the day safely.

But avoiding the subject does not make the risk disappear.

And unlike many retirement risks, long-term care can affect far more than money.

It can affect your spouse. Your children. Where you live. Your independence. Your dignity. Your family's time. Your family's finances. Your legacy. Your ability to give. And the emotional well-being of everyone involved.

That is why long-term care planning is not simply an insurance conversation.

It is a family planning conversation.

And for the Christian household, I believe it is also a stewardship conversation.

The question should begin not with:

"What policy should I buy?"

but with:

"If I need care someday, what do I want that care to look like—and how do I protect the people I love while receiving it?"

Only then should we ask how to pay for it.

Long-Term Care Is Not Just A Nursing Home

One of the biggest misconceptions about long-term care is that it automatically means nursing-home care.

It does not.

Long-term care can happen in many places:

At home.

In an assisted-living community.

In a memory-care setting.

Through adult day services.

In a skilled nursing facility.

Or through a combination of several types of care over time.

A person may begin by needing help a few hours each week.

Later, that person may need daily assistance.

Eventually, round-the-clock supervision may be necessary.

So when we talk about long-term care, we are really talking about a spectrum of support.

That distinction matters because the personal and financial consequences can be very different.

Start With The Care Plan

Before discussing insurance or assets, imagine the situation.

You are 82 years old.

You need help every day.

Where would you want to receive care?

At home?

Near your children?

In a retirement community?

Would you be comfortable in assisted living?

Would your spouse be able to help?

Would your children live nearby?

Would they have jobs?

Children of their own?

Health issues of their own?

These questions matter because people often build long-term-care plans around assumptions that are not realistic.

"My daughter will take care of me."

Maybe.

But is that what your daughter expects?

Can she leave work?

Does she live three states away?

Does she have young children?

Does she know she is part of the plan?

A plan is not a plan if the people responsible for carrying it out do not know it exists.

The Hidden Cost Of Family Care

Family members provide enormous amounts of unpaid care.

And that can be a beautiful expression of love.

But unpaid does not mean costless.

Suppose an adult daughter begins caring for her mother.

She may reduce her work hours.

Turn down a promotion.

Take unpaid leave.

Drive to appointments.

Coordinate medications.

Handle bills.

Prepare meals.

Help with personal care.

Arrange home-care services.

Spend less time with her own spouse and children.

Experience emotional and physical exhaustion.

None of those costs may appear on the retiree's bank statement.

But they are real.

That is why long-term care planning is not only about protecting assets.

It is also about protecting relationships.

"I Don't Want To Be A Burden"

This is one of the most common things people tell me when discussing retirement.

"I don't want to be a burden on my children."

Usually, that statement means much more than money.

It means:

I don't want my children fighting over what to do.

I don't want them quitting their jobs to care for me.

I don't want them paying my bills.

I don't want them feeling guilty.

I don't want them making impossible decisions during a crisis.

I don't want every visit with my grandchildren to become a care meeting.

Long-term care planning cannot eliminate every difficulty.

But it can reduce unnecessary burdens.

And there is an important biblical connection here.

Scripture repeatedly teaches responsibility toward family. First Timothy 5:8 speaks strongly about providing for one's household. We often apply that principle to parents providing for children or spouses providing for one another.

But later in life, providing for family can also mean preparing for our own needs so that those needs do not unnecessarily consume the lives and resources of the people we love.

That does not mean refusing help.

Families care for one another.

Sometimes receiving care graciously is itself an act of love.

The objective is not to become so fiercely independent that we refuse to need anyone.

The objective is to prepare wisely so that love, rather than financial panic, can guide the decisions.

Protect The Healthy Spouse

One of the most important long-term-care questions is often overlooked.

What happens to the spouse who does not need care?

Imagine a married couple.

One spouse requires several years of expensive care.

The other remains healthy.

The financial problem is not simply:

"How do we pay for care?"

It is:

"How do we pay for care without destroying the healthy spouse's retirement?"

The healthy spouse still needs housing.

Food.

Transportation.

Healthcare.

Income.

Financial security.

A future.

Perhaps that spouse still wants to travel.

Give to church.

Help grandchildren.

Remain in the family home.

Live another twenty years.

If the entire financial plan is consumed caring for one spouse, we may have solved one problem by creating another.

This is why long-term care is fundamentally a survivor and family-security issue.

The Good Samaritan And The Cost Of Care

The parable of the Good Samaritan in Luke 10 is fundamentally a lesson about loving our neighbor, not an insurance-planning lesson.

But notice something practical in the story.

Compassion became action.

The Samaritan did not merely feel concern.

He stopped.

He helped.

He used his own resources.

He arranged ongoing care.

There is an important principle there.

Caring for people often requires resources.

Time.

Money.

Transportation.

A place to stay.

Professional assistance.

Attention.

Planning does not replace compassion.

It can make compassionate care more possible.

If we have resources available when care is needed, the family may have more choices about how that care is delivered.

That is one reason we prepare.

Dignity Matters

Long-term care planning can easily become a discussion about numbers.

How much does care cost?

How much insurance should we buy?

How much can we self-fund?

But behind the numbers is a person.

A person who may be frightened.

Embarrassed.

Confused.

Frustrated.

Dependent on others in ways they never expected.

Dignity matters.

One of the purposes of financial planning is to preserve as much choice as reasonably possible.

Where do you receive care?

Who provides it?

Can you stay home longer?

Can your spouse remain financially secure?

Can your children be your children rather than becoming your full-time care managers?

Money cannot guarantee dignity.

But resources and preparation can create options.

Self-Funding Long-Term Care

One strategy is to self-fund.

In other words, if care is needed, you pay for it from your own resources.

That might include:

Cash.

Investment accounts.

Retirement accounts.

Income.

Home equity.

Other assets.

For households with substantial financial resources, self-funding may be reasonable.

But do not stop the analysis at:

"We have enough money."

Ask:

Which assets would pay for care?

What tax consequences would withdrawals create?

What if markets are down?

What happens to the healthy spouse?

How many years of care could the plan absorb?

What happens to the legacy?

What happens to charitable goals?

Would paying for care force the sale of assets at an undesirable time?

What happens if both spouses eventually need care?

Self-funding does not mean ignoring the risk.

It means intentionally retaining the risk.

That is very different.

Traditional Long-Term Care Insurance

Traditional long-term care insurance is designed specifically to transfer some portion of long-term-care risk to an insurance company, subject to the policy's terms.

Policies can vary substantially.

Potential considerations include:

Daily or monthly benefit amounts.

Benefit periods.

Elimination periods.

Inflation protection.

Covered services.

Home-care provisions.

Shared-care features.

Premium structure.

Underwriting.

Benefit triggers.

Insurance-company strength.

Traditional coverage can be valuable for some households because it allows them to transfer a potentially large risk.

But it also raises questions.

What will premiums cost?

Can premiums increase under the contract and applicable rules?

Will the policy still be affordable later?

What happens if care is never needed?

How much risk should actually be insured?

The answer depends on the household.

Again:

Start with the risk.

Not the product.

Hybrid Life And Long-Term Care Strategies

Some people dislike traditional long-term-care insurance because they worry:

"What if I pay premiums for years and never need care?"

That concern has contributed to the popularity of hybrid strategies.

Depending on the contract, a hybrid product may combine life insurance with long-term-care benefits or provide access to a death benefit under qualifying long-term-care or chronic-illness provisions.

The basic appeal is understandable.

If care is needed, benefits may be available under the contract.

If care is not needed, a death benefit may eventually pass to beneficiaries, subject to the policy terms.

This can potentially turn one pool of money into a resource serving multiple possible purposes.

Care.

Protection.

Legacy.

That is where the concept of asset leverage becomes important.

Asset Leverage, Not Just Insurance

Remember one of the themes we established earlier in the book.

A financial tool should not be evaluated only by asking:

"How much tax does this save?"

or:

"What return does this earn?"

We should also ask:

"How many legitimate objectives can this resource accomplish efficiently?"

A properly structured permanent life insurance strategy, depending on the policy and circumstances, might potentially help:

Protect a surviving spouse.

Create a death benefit.

Provide legacy leverage.

Provide charitable leverage.

Create liquidity.

And, with appropriate contractual provisions, potentially provide access to benefits if qualifying care needs arise.

That does not make permanent life insurance automatically appropriate.

It means the tool deserves to be evaluated based on the jobs it may perform.

This is especially relevant when a household already wants to leave money behind.

Suppose Mark and Lisa intend to leave $500,000 to children, church, and charities.

If they simply reserve $500,000 of investment assets for that purpose, those assets remain exposed to the other demands of retirement.

But perhaps another financial structure could create the intended legacy while allowing other assets to remain available for retirement.

That is leverage.

The right answer depends on the actual economics, guarantees, underwriting, liquidity, costs, tax rules, and policy provisions.

But the planning question is worth asking.

Protection, Leverage, And Efficiency

This is the distinction I want readers to understand before we reach the later strategic-planning chapters.

Insurance and estate-planning tools are not merely about avoiding taxes.

They may be about:

Risk transfer.

Asset protection.

Income protection.

Liquidity.

Legacy leverage.

Care funding.

Family security.

Charitable impact.

Tax efficiency.

And coordination.

Sometimes paying a premium today can protect a much larger financial objective later.

Sometimes keeping assets liquid is better.

Sometimes self-funding is better.

Sometimes a hybrid strategy creates useful leverage.

The goal is not to own more products.

The goal is to make the entire balance sheet work harder and more intelligently.

What About Chronic-Illness Riders?

Permanent life insurance policies may offer different types of riders or provisions related to chronic illness or long-term care.

These are not all the same.

The contractual definitions matter.

Benefit triggers matter.

Reimbursement versus indemnity structures may matter.

The effect on the remaining death benefit matters.

Charges matter.

Tax treatment can depend on applicable law and circumstances.

Never assume that a rider marketed as helping with long-term care is identical to a traditional long-term-care policy.

Read the contract.

Understand what triggers benefits.

Understand what happens to the death benefit.

Understand what is guaranteed.

This book is about planning principles, not recommending a specific insurance contract.

The principle is simple:

If one asset can efficiently help protect against a care event while also supporting a legitimate legacy objective, it may deserve consideration.

Home Equity Is Part Of The Balance Sheet

For many retirees, the home is one of their largest assets.

Yet it is often excluded from long-term-care planning.

"We're never selling the house."

Maybe not.

But if circumstances change, home equity may become a significant financial resource.

Possible strategies could involve:

Selling and downsizing.

Moving to a community better suited to aging.

Using equity strategically.

Leaving the home untouched and relying on other assets.

The right answer depends on goals.

But ignoring home equity because "we'd never sell the house" may remove a significant resource from the plan without examining the tradeoff.

And there is another question.

Is the home itself appropriate for aging?

Stairs?

Bathrooms?

Doorways?

Maintenance?

Distance from family?

Distance from medical care?

Transportation?

Sometimes the best long-term-care decision is not an insurance decision at all.

It is a housing decision made ten years earlier.

Medicaid Is Not The Same As Medicare

This distinction is important.

Medicare and Medicaid are different programs.

Medicare does not cover long-term custodial care when that is the only care needed. It may cover limited skilled nursing or home-health services when specific requirements are met.

Medicaid may provide long-term-care assistance for qualifying individuals, but eligibility rules involve financial and other requirements and can vary by state and circumstance.

Planning around Medicaid can involve complex legal issues.

Do not transfer assets or restructure ownership based on something you heard from a friend.

If Medicaid planning may be relevant, work with a qualified elder-law attorney familiar with the rules in your state.

This is an area where professional guidance matters.

The Faith Question Is Not "How Much Can I Keep?"

A faith-based long-term-care plan should not become:

"How do I protect every dollar so someone else pays for my care?"

That misses the point.

Nor should it become:

"I should spend everything because money doesn't matter."

That misses the point too.

The better stewardship question is:

"What resources have we been given, what responsibilities do we have, and how can we structure those resources so that care can be provided without unnecessarily harming the people and purposes we value?"

That may mean spending your own money.

Buying insurance.

Using home equity.

Accepting help from family.

Using public benefits for which you legitimately qualify.

Or combining several approaches.

Stewardship is not defined by which tool pays the bill.

It is defined by the wisdom and integrity with which the plan is built.

Caring For Parents While Preparing For Yourself

Many people approaching retirement are already experiencing long-term care from the other side.

They are caring for aging parents.

Maybe you are doing that now.

If so, pay attention.

What has been difficult?

What do you wish your parents had discussed earlier?

Which documents were hard to find?

What financial decisions created stress?

What worked well?

What would you want done differently for your own children?

Sometimes caring for parents gives us the clearest possible picture of why our own planning matters.

Use that experience.

Do not repeat avoidable problems.

Honoring Father And Mother

Scripture's command to honor father and mother has meaning throughout life.

For many adults, that eventually includes helping aging parents.

But honoring a parent does not necessarily mean personally providing every hour of care.

Sometimes the most loving decision is arranging professional assistance.

Sometimes it means helping with finances.

Transportation.

Housing.

Advocacy.

Medical appointments.

Or simply being present.

Families have different resources and circumstances.

The goal should not be guilt.

It should be thoughtful care.

And if we want our own children to be free to love us rather than feel trapped by our care needs, preparing in advance can be one way we extend that same grace to them.

The Caregiver Needs Care Too

This deserves its own section.

Caregivers often become invisible.

Everyone asks:

"How is Dad?"

Far fewer people ask:

"How is Mom doing while taking care of Dad?"

The caregiver may experience:

Exhaustion.

Isolation.

Stress.

Lost income.

Physical strain.

Depression.

Guilt.

Financial pressure.

A strong long-term-care plan should protect the caregiver too.

That may mean budgeting for respite care.

Professional home care.

Adult day services.

Housekeeping.

Transportation.

Meal support.

Or other assistance.

If the plan assumes the healthy spouse will provide unlimited unpaid care indefinitely, we may not really have a plan.

We may have an expectation.

Those are different.

What Would Jesus' Example Of Service Ask Of Us?

Earlier we discussed Jesus washing the disciples' feet in John 13.

It is one of Scripture's clearest pictures of humble service.

Long-term care can require that kind of humility on both sides.

The humility to serve someone who can no longer care for themselves.

And the humility to allow someone else to serve us.

That second part can be difficult.

People who have spent their entire lives providing for others may struggle deeply with dependence.

"I don't want anyone helping me."

"I don't want my children seeing me like this."

"I should be able to do this myself."

But there may come a season when receiving care is part of life.

Our objective is not to pretend that dependence can always be avoided.

It is to preserve dignity, choice, and relationships when dependence arrives.

What Is Enough For Long-Term Care?

The question of "enough" returns here too.

How much money should be reserved for a possible care event?

Enough to cover one year?

Three years?

Five?

An unlimited amount?

There is no universal answer.

If you reserve every possible dollar for a care event that may never happen, you may sacrifice:

Travel.

Giving.

Family experiences.

Mission.

Enjoyment.

Other retirement goals.

If you reserve nothing, you may expose the household to unnecessary risk.

The objective is balance.

How much can we reasonably self-fund?

How much risk would materially threaten the plan?

Could that larger risk be transferred?

What resources are already available?

What would happen to the healthy spouse?

Those questions create a much better answer than simply choosing an arbitrary number.

Don't Let Fear Steal The Healthy Years

This is important.

A long-term-care plan should create confidence.

Not fear.

Imagine someone refusing to travel at 67 because:

"What if I need nursing care at 87?"

That may not be prudent.

It may simply be fear.

We plan for the possibility of future care so that we can live today with greater confidence.

Set aside appropriate resources.

Transfer risk where appropriate.

Communicate with family.

Prepare legal documents.

Then go live.

The purpose of long-term-care planning is not to make aging the center of retirement.

It is to prevent fear of aging from becoming the center of retirement.

Legal Documents Matter

Money alone is not enough.

A strong care plan should coordinate with legal planning.

Depending on your circumstances and state law, that may include documents such as:

A durable financial power of attorney.

Healthcare power of attorney or healthcare proxy.

Advance medical directive.

HIPAA authorizations.

Trust documents where appropriate.

Other estate-planning documents.

The exact documents and terminology vary.

Work with a qualified attorney.

But understand the purpose.

If you cannot make decisions, someone needs legal authority to act.

Without proper documents, a family may face unnecessary delays, costs, or court involvement during an already difficult time.

Simplify Before Someone Else Has To Take Over

There is another practical form of stewardship.

Simplification.

How many bank accounts do you have?

Investment accounts?

Old retirement plans?

Insurance policies?

Credit cards?

Online accounts?

Properties?

Subscriptions?

Does your spouse know where everything is?

Could an adult child find it?

Could your financial agent under a power of attorney understand it?

A complicated financial life may be manageable while you are healthy.

It can become a nightmare when someone else has to take over.

Retirement can be an excellent time to simplify.

Not because simplicity is always financially optimal.

Because manageability has value.

The Family Meeting

Consider having a family meeting before care is needed.

Not to disclose every dollar if you are uncomfortable doing so.

But to discuss the plan.

You might explain:

Where you would prefer to live.

Who holds healthcare authority.

Who holds financial authority.

Where important documents are stored.

Which professionals should be contacted.

What insurance exists.

How care is intended to be funded.

Whether you have preferences regarding home care or a community.

What role, if any, you hope children will play.

This conversation can prevent enormous confusion later.

And it allows your children to say something important too:

"That plan isn't realistic for us."

Better to learn that at 68 than during a crisis at 88.

Mark And Lisa Choose A Strategy

Let's return to Mark and Lisa.

They review several possible approaches.

They could purchase traditional long-term-care insurance.

They could use a hybrid strategy.

They could self-fund entirely.

Or they could combine insurance with personal assets.

After analyzing their resources, they determine that they could comfortably self-fund the first portion of a care need.

But they do not want an extended care event to threaten Lisa's income if Mark needs care first—or Mark's income if Lisa needs care first.

They also want to leave something to their children and continue supporting their church and charitable causes.

That changes the analysis.

They are no longer asking only:

"How do we pay for long-term care?"

They are asking:

"How do we pay for care while protecting the healthy spouse and preserving the other purposes these assets are supposed to serve?"

Perhaps they retain a meaningful pool of liquid assets for early care needs.

Perhaps they transfer part of the larger catastrophic risk through insurance.

Perhaps permanent insurance with appropriate care provisions deserves evaluation because they already have a legacy objective.

Perhaps it does not.

The numbers will determine that.

But notice what they did not do.

They did not ask:

"What long-term-care policy should we buy?"

They asked:

"What financial and family risk are we trying to solve?"

That question leads to a much better conversation.

The Best Long-Term Care Plan May Be A Family Plan

Long-term care is not just about dollars.

It is about people.

The spouse who becomes the caregiver.

The daughter who lives nearby.

The son who manages the finances.

The grandchildren who want time with you without every visit becoming a medical meeting.

The professionals helping your family.

The decisions you make while you are still able to make them.

That is why I believe a strong long-term-care plan has three parts:

A care plan.

A financial plan.

A communication plan.

Miss any one of those, and the others become harder.

Your Purpose Driven Long-Term Care & Family Exercise

Sit down with your spouse, partner, or family and answer these questions.

1. Where would I want to receive care?

At home?

Near family?

In a community?

2. Who do I assume will help me?

Have I actually discussed that with them?

3. If my spouse needs care first, what happens to my financial security?

4. If I need care first, what happens to theirs?

5. How much of the risk could we comfortably self-fund?

6. Which assets would we use?

7. What happens if the care need lasts much longer than expected?

8. Would insurance improve the plan?

9. Have we evaluated traditional and hybrid options if appropriate?

10. Do any existing life insurance policies contain long-term-care or chronic-illness provisions?

Do we understand exactly how they work?

11. Is our current home suitable for aging?

12. If we need to move, where would we go?

13. Who has financial power of attorney?

14. Who can make healthcare decisions?

15. Does our family know what we want?

16. Are our financial affairs simple enough for someone else to manage?

17. If a child is part of the care plan, have we actually asked whether that role is realistic?

18. What resources are specifically intended to protect the healthy spouse?

19. What legacy and charitable goals do we want to preserve even if care is needed?

20. Complete this sentence:

"If one of us needs care, we want our plan to protect..."

Do not answer only:

"Our money."

Think bigger.

Our spouse.

Our children.

Our dignity.

Our independence.

Our choices.

Our relationships.

Our legacy.

Our ability to continue giving.

The answers are more important than the product.

Dignity, Choice, And Independence

Why do we plan for long-term care?

Not because we are pessimistic.

Not because we assume something terrible will happen.

We plan because resources create choices.

If you need care:

Where do you want to receive it?

Who do you want helping you?

How much independence can you preserve?

What burden do you want to avoid placing on your spouse?

What burden do you want to avoid placing on your children?

What other purposes do you want your financial resources to continue serving?

Those are Purpose Driven Retirement questions.

The money is simply what gives you options.

Protect More Than The Portfolio

When long-term care is discussed solely as a threat to retirement assets, we miss the bigger picture.

Yes, care can be expensive.

But the greater risk may be:

A spouse becoming exhausted.

Children fighting over decisions.

Someone quitting a career to provide care.

A family making choices in panic.

Assets being sold at the wrong time.

Medical wishes being unclear.

A retiree ending up somewhere they never wanted to be.

A lifetime of charitable intentions disappearing because no contingency plan existed.

Good planning cannot guarantee none of those things will happen.

But it can make many of them less likely.

Have The Conversation While You Can

There may come a day when long-term-care decisions have to be made quickly.

Do not let that be the first time your family discusses them.

Tell the people you love what you want.

Ask what they can realistically do.

Put the legal documents in place.

Understand the financial resources.

Review insurance.

Think about housing.

Simplify the financial life.

Then put the plan away and go enjoy retirement.

Because this chapter is not supposed to make you afraid of getting older.

It is supposed to help you prepare wisely enough that fear does not control the years before you get there.

From Protection To Legacy

We have now spent several chapters protecting the retirement plan.

Healthcare.

Long-term care.

The healthy spouse.

Family.

Independence.

But protection is only part of stewardship.

Eventually we need to ask another question:

What happens to everything we have built when we no longer need it?

Who receives it?

Family?

Children?

Grandchildren?

Church?

Charity?

A ministry?

A combination?

And can we structure those assets so they do more than simply pass from one account to another?

Can they protect?

Leverage?

Give?

Teach?

Serve?

And continue a mission after our own lifetime?

That is where we are going next.

Part V — Provide, Protect, Leverage, and Pass It On

◆

These tools are not merely about tax mitigation. They are about protection, asset leverage, efficiency, family responsibility, generosity, and directing resources toward the people and purposes that matter.

Chapter 11

Life Insurance, Asset Leverage, and the People You Love

Protection First. Leverage Second. Legacy With Purpose.

Life Insurance Is About People Before It Is About Money

Life insurance is often introduced as a financial product. Premiums. Death benefits. Cash values. Riders. Rates of return. Tax treatment. All of those things can matter. But none of them should be the starting point.

The starting point should be a person.

Who would be financially affected if you died? What promises have you made? What responsibilities would remain? What income would disappear? What dreams would become harder for the people you love?

That is why life insurance belongs in a Purpose Driven Retirement plan. It is not primarily about creating a pile of money at death. It is about creating resources at a moment when the people you love may need them most.

First Timothy 5:8 speaks forcefully about providing for one's household. The verse is not an insurance recommendation, but the principle of family responsibility is difficult to miss. Providing for family is not limited to what we do while we are alive. Thoughtful planning asks whether the people who depend on us would still be protected if we were no longer here.

Protection Comes Before Performance

People sometimes evaluate life insurance by asking, "What return will I get?" That can be a useful question in the right context, especially when evaluating permanent insurance. But it is not the first question.

A homeowner does not usually buy fire insurance because the policy has an attractive return. The policy exists because the financial consequence of a fire could be devastating.

Life insurance begins the same way. Identify the risk first. Then decide whether transferring some of that risk to an insurance company improves the plan.

Ask what must be protected: a spouse's income, a mortgage, dependent children, a business, estate liquidity, charitable commitments, a pension survivor need, future care costs, or a legacy objective. Only after the need is clear should we discuss which type of policy—if any—fits the job.

Term Insurance: Simple Protection for a Defined Need

Term life insurance is designed primarily to provide death-benefit protection for a stated period. For many families, that simplicity is exactly what is needed.

A household may need substantial coverage while children are young, a mortgage is large, retirement assets are still being accumulated, or one spouse remains heavily dependent on the other's earnings. If the need is temporary, temporary insurance may be appropriate.

The question is not whether term insurance is "better" or "worse" than permanent insurance. The question is whether the duration of the insurance matches the duration of the need.

If the financial obligation is likely to disappear, term coverage can be an efficient solution. If the objective is expected to remain for life—such as estate liquidity, lifelong survivor protection, charitable legacy, or a permanent inheritance objective—then permanent coverage may deserve consideration.

Permanent Life Insurance: A Different Kind of Tool

Permanent life insurance is intended, subject to the contract and continued funding requirements, to provide coverage beyond a limited term. Depending on the type of policy, it may also include cash value and other contractual features.

That makes permanent insurance a different planning tool. It may potentially serve several legitimate objectives at once: survivor protection, estate liquidity, legacy creation, charitable leverage, access to cash value under policy terms, and—when appropriate riders or provisions are included—potential access to benefits following qualifying chronic-illness or long-term-care events.

But permanent insurance is not automatically superior because it can perform more jobs. More features usually mean more complexity. Costs, guarantees, assumptions, surrender provisions, policy performance, underwriting, insurer strength, tax rules, and funding requirements all matter.

The rule remains the same: purpose first, product second.

Asset Leverage: Making One Dollar Serve More Than One Purpose

This is where I want to introduce a concept that will continue throughout Part V: asset leverage.

Asset leverage does not mean simply borrowing money or taking greater investment risk. In this context, it means asking whether an asset or planning strategy can efficiently support more than one objective.

Suppose a couple intends to leave $500,000 to their children and church. One approach is to mentally reserve $500,000 of investments and hope those assets remain available at death. Another approach may be to evaluate whether a portion of current assets or cash flow can be repositioned into a strategy designed to create a defined death benefit.

The second approach is not automatically better. The economics must work. Liquidity matters. Health and insurability matter. Guarantees matter. The policy must be properly structured and monitored.

But the planning question is powerful: can we protect the family, preserve other assets for retirement, create liquidity, and support legacy goals with greater efficiency than simply leaving a pool of money untouched?

That is asset leverage.

Life Insurance Is Not Just About Tax Mitigation

Life insurance is sometimes presented almost entirely through its tax characteristics. That is too narrow.

Tax treatment can be important. Under current federal law, life insurance death benefits are often received by beneficiaries without federal income tax, subject to important exceptions and individual circumstances. Cash-value access can also have tax implications, and poorly structured distributions, loans, lapses, or modified endowment contracts can create very different outcomes.

Those rules deserve professional analysis. But even when tax benefits are available, taxes should not become the entire reason for the strategy.

The larger questions are protection, leverage, liquidity, efficiency, control, and purpose.

A strategy that saves tax but creates the wrong insurance commitment is not good planning. A strategy that provides needed protection and creates useful leverage may be valuable even when tax savings are not the primary benefit.

Protecting a Surviving Spouse

Retirement planning often focuses on the day both spouses retire. But every married retirement plan should eventually model a second date: the day one spouse is gone.

What income disappears? Does a pension decline? Does one Social Security benefit disappear? Do tax brackets change? Does the survivor remain in the home? Are there debts? Will healthcare costs change?

The surviving spouse may have fewer income sources while many expenses remain.

Life insurance can sometimes create a pool of capital designed specifically for that transition. The death benefit may help replace lost income, create a reserve, pay debt, provide time to make decisions, or reduce pressure to sell investments during an unfavorable market.

The point is not to make the survivor wealthy. The point is to preserve choices.

Pension Maximization Requires Care

Some retirees are offered a larger pension if they elect a single-life benefit rather than a survivor benefit. A strategy sometimes called pension maximization uses some of the higher pension income to purchase life insurance for the spouse.

Conceptually, the idea can sound attractive: take the larger pension, use part of the difference for insurance, and potentially leave the surviving spouse a lump sum.

But this strategy requires careful analysis. Is the retiree insurable? What does the insurance cost? What is guaranteed? How long must premiums be paid? Could the policy lapse? How much death benefit is truly required? Would the death benefit realistically replace the lost pension? Does the pension have a cost-of-living adjustment? Are other benefits tied to the survivor election?

For federal employees and others with complex benefit systems, survivor elections can interact with healthcare or other benefits. The pension and insurance must be evaluated together. Life insurance should never be casually presented as an automatic substitute for a survivor pension.

Long-Term Care and Chronic-Illness Features

In Chapter 10 we discussed how some permanent policies may contain long-term-care or chronic-illness riders or provisions. This is one of the clearest examples of multi-purpose planning.

A household may already want permanent death-benefit protection. If an appropriately structured policy can also provide contractual access to benefits following a qualifying care event, the same planning resource may potentially address both legacy and care risk.

But the details matter enormously. Long-term-care riders and chronic-illness riders are not interchangeable. Benefit triggers, reimbursement or indemnity structures, acceleration formulas, charges, remaining death benefits, tax treatment, and contractual guarantees can differ.

Do not buy a policy because a brochure says it "covers long-term care." Understand precisely what the contract does.

A Legacy Is More Than an Inheritance

Proverbs 13:22 says that a good person leaves an inheritance to children's children. That verse is sometimes reduced to a command to accumulate as much money as possible. I do not think that captures the full idea of biblical legacy.

An inheritance can include financial resources. It can also include faith, wisdom, character, opportunity, education, generosity, family stories, and an example worth following.

Money is one part of legacy. It is not the whole legacy.

That distinction protects us from turning wealth accumulation into its own form of worship. The goal is not to die with the largest possible estate. The goal is to use what has been entrusted to us well—during life and after it.

The Warning of the Rich Fool

Jesus' parable of the rich fool in Luke 12 provides an important counterweight to financial planning. The man's land produced abundantly. He built larger barns, accumulated more, and told himself he had plenty stored up for many years.

The problem was not that he planned. The problem was that accumulation had become the destination. His wealth was centered on himself, and he had lost sight of the larger purpose of life.

Retirement planning can fall into the same trap.

One more million. One more account. One more year of work. One more percentage point of return.

Eventually we must ask: enough for what?

Financial security matters. Providing for family matters. Prudence matters. But if the plan becomes nothing more than building larger barns, we may arrive at retirement financially prepared and spiritually empty.

What Is Enough?

This may be one of the most important questions in the entire book.

What is enough?

Enough income to live with dignity. Enough reserve to handle uncertainty. Enough protection for a spouse. Enough flexibility for healthcare. Enough to enjoy the life you worked for. Enough to help family responsibly. Enough to give generously.

But after "enough" is reasonably established, what happens to the excess?

Does every additional dollar need to become more personal consumption? More accumulation? A larger estate?

Or could some of it become impact?

The answer will be different for every household. The purpose of asking is not to create guilt. It is to prevent accumulation from becoming automatic.

Life Insurance and Charitable Leverage

Suppose giving to your church, ministry, school, community organization, or another charity has been important throughout your life. You may want that generosity to continue after you are gone.

Life insurance can sometimes be incorporated into charitable planning. Depending on ownership, beneficiary structure, tax law, insurable-interest rules, and the specific strategy, insurance may help create a charitable gift larger than the dollars contributed during life.

That can be another form of leverage.

But charitable insurance planning can become technically complex. Ownership and beneficiary decisions can have legal and tax consequences. Work with qualified tax, legal, insurance, and financial professionals before implementing a strategy.

And remember: the charitable objective comes first. The tax deduction, if available, is a planning benefit—not the mission.

Give While You Are Here, Too

A death benefit can create a meaningful legacy. But do not let planning for generosity at death replace generosity during life.

Second Corinthians 9:7 emphasizes giving willingly rather than reluctantly or under compulsion. That spirit matters.

Maybe part of the plan is a future gift through life insurance. Maybe another part is giving today.

Support the church now. Help the family now. Take the mission trip now. Fund the scholarship now. Mentor the person now. Buy the meal now.

There is something powerful about seeing the impact of generosity while you are still here to participate in it.

Life Insurance Can Create Equalization

Families do not always own assets that divide neatly.

Perhaps one child will inherit a family business. Another has no interest in it. Perhaps one child receives family property while another lives across the country. Perhaps a large charitable gift is important, but parents also want children to receive an inheritance.

Life insurance can sometimes create liquidity that helps equalize an estate without forcing the sale of an illiquid asset.

That does not mean every child must receive mathematically identical value. Fair and equal are not always the same. But insurance can provide another tool when the family wants to balance competing objectives.

Do Not Sacrifice Retirement to Manufacture a Legacy

This principle is essential.

Your retirement assets exist first to support your retirement.

Do not become insurance-rich and cash-poor. Do not commit so much money to premiums that you cannot travel, give, handle emergencies, or maintain adequate liquidity. Do not preserve an inheritance at the expense of necessary healthcare or your spouse's security.

A legacy strategy should strengthen the retirement plan, not suffocate it.

The biblical call to provide for others does not require reckless self-neglect. Wise stewardship requires balance.

Policy Design Matters

Two life insurance policies with the same death benefit can behave very differently.

Depending on the policy type, important considerations may include guarantees, premium duration, cash-value assumptions, credited rates or investment performance, surrender charges, policy loans, cost-of-insurance charges, dividend assumptions, riders, underwriting class, and the financial strength and claims-paying ability of the insurer.

Illustrations are not guarantees unless a value is specifically identified as guaranteed.

If a policy depends on non-guaranteed assumptions, ask what happens if those assumptions are lower than illustrated.

Permanent life insurance should be reviewed periodically. A policy purchased twenty years ago should not automatically be assumed to be performing exactly as originally expected.

Beneficiary Designations Are Part of the Plan

A beautifully designed policy can still fail the family if the beneficiary designation does not reflect current intentions.

Marriage, divorce, births, deaths, trusts, charitable goals, and family circumstances change.

Review beneficiaries periodically and coordinate them with the estate plan. The will does not necessarily control assets that pass by beneficiary designation.

The paperwork must tell the same story as the plan.

Ownership Matters Too

Who owns the policy can affect control, estate planning, taxation, access to cash value, and other outcomes. In some situations, trusts or other ownership structures may be considered.

This is not an area for casual do-it-yourself planning when substantial assets or complex objectives are involved.

The financial planner, insurance professional, attorney, and tax professional should understand what the others are trying to accomplish.

Coordination is part of stewardship.

Mark and Lisa Put Purpose Before Product

Let's return to Mark and Lisa.

They want several things. They want the surviving spouse financially secure. They want resources available if a major care event occurs. They want their children to inherit something, but they do not want inheritance to become the center of their children's lives. They want their church to benefit from the values they supported together. And they want enough liquidity to enjoy retirement while they are healthy.

They could simply leave their investments alone and hope enough remains.

Instead, they ask a different set of questions.

How much does the survivor actually need? Which risks are temporary and which are permanent? How much liquidity must remain accessible? Is there a permanent legacy objective? Could insurance transfer a risk more efficiently than retaining it? Could one strategy help protect the spouse, support care planning, and create legacy leverage? What are the costs and tradeoffs?

Only after answering those questions do they evaluate policies.

That order matters.

They are not buying insurance and searching for a reason to justify it. They are defining the mission of their assets and determining whether insurance deserves a role.

Your Purpose Driven Protection & Leverage Exercise

Before discussing a specific policy, answer these questions:

1. Who would be financially affected if I died tomorrow?
2. What income would disappear?
3. What debts or obligations would remain?

4. What does my spouse need to remain financially independent?
5. Are my insurance needs temporary, permanent, or both?
6. Do I have a pension or benefit election that changes at death?
7. What role should insurance play in our long-term-care strategy, if any?
8. How much liquidity must remain outside an insurance policy?
9. Do we have a specific inheritance objective—or are we simply assuming we should leave "whatever is left"?
10. What do we want to leave to children or grandchildren?
11. What do we want to leave to church, ministry, charity, or community?
12. Could giving during our lifetime accomplish part of that purpose better?
13. Would insurance create useful leverage, or merely add complexity?
14. Do we understand what is guaranteed and what is not?
15. Could we comfortably maintain the strategy if markets, health, income, or family circumstances change?
16. Are ownership and beneficiary designations coordinated with our estate plan?
17. When was the last time existing policies were reviewed?
18. Complete this sentence: "If our life insurance does its job, it will allow the people and causes we love to..."

That last answer is the purpose of the policy.

Passing It On

Life insurance is ultimately a promise funded in advance.

It says that if life changes before we expect it to, resources will be there for someone else.

For some families, that promise is temporary.

For others, it is permanent.

For some, it protects a spouse.

For others, it helps protect children, a business, a special-needs family member, a church, a charity, or several generations.

The tool is not sacred. The purpose is what matters.

When life insurance is used well, it can be one part of a larger stewardship plan—protecting the people we are responsible for, preserving choices, leveraging assets, and intentionally passing resources toward the people and missions we believe matter.

And that naturally brings us to the next question.

Once we know what we want our resources to accomplish, how do we make sure they actually get there?

That is the work of estate and legacy planning.

Next: Chapter 12 — Estate Planning, Legacy, and Passing on More Than Money

In the next chapter, we will build on the original Purpose Driven Retirement estate-planning framework: wills, trusts, beneficiary designations, incapacity planning, family communication, lifetime giving, charitable planning, and the difference between an estate and a legacy.

But in this edition we will go further. We will ask not only, "Who gets what?" but, "What are we trying to pass on?" Faith. Values. Wisdom. Generosity. Responsibility. Stories. Opportunity. And a mission that can continue beyond our own lifetime.

Chapter 12

Estate Planning, Legacy, and Passing on More Than Money

What Will Continue Because You Were Here?

Estate Planning Begins With a Bigger Question

Most estate-planning conversations begin with documents.

Do you have a will? Do you need a trust? Who is the executor? Who are the beneficiaries?

Those are important questions. But they are not the first questions.

The first question is: What do you want what you have built to accomplish?

Your estate is what you own. Your legacy is what you leave behind.

Those are not the same thing.

Your estate may include a home, retirement accounts, investments, insurance, business interests, and personal property. Your legacy may include faith, values, stories, generosity, relationships, lessons, traditions, opportunity, and an example worth following.

An estate can be measured in dollars. A legacy usually cannot.

A Biblical View of Inheritance

Scripture speaks positively about providing for family and future generations. Proverbs 13:22 tells us that a good person leaves an inheritance to children's children.

But biblical inheritance should not be reduced to a contest over who dies with the largest account balance.

What are we really trying to leave?

Money can create opportunity. It can provide security. It can fund education. It can help a child purchase a home. It can support a family member with special needs. It can continue charitable work.

But money without wisdom can also create problems.

That is why passing on wealth should include passing on the values needed to steward it.

First Take Care of the Life God Has Given You

There is an order to this planning.

First, take care of your life.

Second, protect the people who depend on you.

Third, intentionally direct what remains.

Imagine aggressively giving assets away simply to reduce an estate, only to discover later that you need those resources for healthcare or long-term care.

That does not make sense.

Now imagine preserving every possible dollar for heirs while refusing to enjoy a meaningful trip with your spouse, help a grandchild while you can watch the impact, or support a ministry that matters deeply to you.

That may not make sense either.

Legacy should not require abandoning the life you are still called to live.

Do Not Store Everything in the Barn

The parable of the rich fool in Luke 12 returns here for a reason.

The man accumulated more and more, built larger barns, and assumed his abundance guaranteed the future.

Jesus' warning was not against prudent preparation. It was against allowing accumulation to become the purpose.

Estate planning can become another version of building bigger barns if the only objective is maximizing what remains at death.

The better question is not, "How much can I leave?"

It is, "How can what I have been entrusted with continue doing good?"

A Will Is Important—but It Does Not Control Everything

A will is a foundational estate-planning document for many households.

But some assets may pass outside the will through beneficiary designations, joint ownership, trust provisions, or transfer-on-death and payable-on-death arrangements where applicable.

That means a beautifully drafted will does not guarantee that every asset will transfer according to the plan.

Estate planning is not merely document planning.

It is ownership, beneficiary, tax, insurance, legal, and family coordination.

The Beneficiary Form Can Override the Story You Intended to Tell

Imagine your will says everything should pass to your current spouse.

But an old retirement account still names a former spouse.

Or one child is named on an account while the estate plan intends equal treatment among three children.

Depending on the asset and applicable law, the beneficiary designation may control.

Review retirement accounts, life insurance, annuities, bank accounts, investment accounts, and other assets with beneficiary or transfer provisions.

The paperwork should tell the same story as your intentions.

Estate Planning Is Also About Incapacity

People often think estate planning begins when they die.

Some of its most important protections may be needed while they are alive.

If you cannot make decisions, who handles your finances? Who pays bills? Who communicates with financial institutions? Who manages investments? Who deals with insurance? Who makes healthcare decisions?

That is why powers of attorney, healthcare directives, and other appropriate legal documents can be every bit as important as the will.

Estate planning is also about protecting you during life.

The Person You Choose Matters

A legal document can give someone authority. It cannot give that person judgment.

The person you love most is not automatically the person best equipped for every role.

An agent, trustee, executor, or personal representative may need to manage money, keep records, work with professionals, resolve family conflict, and honor your wishes even when they personally disagree.

Different people may be appropriate for different responsibilities.

Choose thoughtfully rather than automatically.

Do Not Leave a Treasure Hunt

One of the greatest gifts you can leave your family is organization.

Imagine losing a spouse and then having to discover where the insurance policy is, who manages the investments, whether a survivor pension exists, where passwords are stored, whether there is a trust, who the attorney is, and which bills are automatically paid.

Grief is difficult enough.

Do not add an unnecessary financial scavenger hunt.

Create an organized inventory. Keep it secure. Make sure the appropriate people know how to access what they will need.

The Most Tax-Efficient Asset May Depend on Who Receives It

Suppose you intend to leave assets to children, grandchildren, and charity.

Should each beneficiary receive the same percentage of every account?

Not necessarily.

Different assets can create different tax consequences for different beneficiaries. Tax-deferred retirement assets, taxable investments, Roth assets, real estate, and life insurance can have different characteristics under applicable law.

In some circumstances, an asset that is less efficient for an individual heir may be especially useful for a charitable beneficiary.

The principle is simple: who receives an asset can matter almost as much as which asset they receive.

This is another place where estate planning and lifetime tax planning should communicate.

Charity as Part of the Estate Plan

If giving has been important throughout your life, there is no reason generosity must automatically stop when your life ends.

Perhaps you have supported a church, ministry, school, hospital, scholarship, community organization, or another cause.

Your estate plan can allow that work to continue.

But begin with purpose.

Why does the organization matter to you? What do you want the gift to accomplish? Would giving during life be more meaningful? Would you like children or grandchildren involved? Could the gift be structured more efficiently?

The tax benefit, if one exists, is secondary.

The mission comes first.

Donor-Advised Funds: Creating a Family Practice of Generosity

A donor-advised fund can sometimes do more than organize charitable gifts.

It can become a family teaching tool.

Imagine establishing a charitable account and gathering children or grandchildren once a year. Each person researches a cause. They explain why it matters. The family decides together where grants should go.

Now a financial tool is accomplishing several purposes at once: charitable giving, possible tax efficiency, family involvement, education, and the transmission of values.

That is asset leverage applied to generosity.

The account is useful. The family practice may be the greater legacy.

Charitable Trusts and Strategic Giving

For some households, charitable trusts or other advanced charitable arrangements may help coordinate giving with income, estate, tax, diversification, or legacy objectives.

These strategies can be powerful, but they can also be complex and highly dependent on current law and individual circumstances.

Do not begin with, "We need a charitable trust."

Begin with, "We want to accomplish this charitable objective while also protecting these family and retirement needs."

Then let qualified legal, tax, and financial professionals determine whether a trust or another strategy improves the plan.

Purpose first. Structure second.

Life Insurance and Charitable Legacy

As we discussed in Chapter 11, life insurance may sometimes create legacy leverage.

A household that wants to make a meaningful future gift may evaluate whether insurance can help create a defined charitable benefit while preserving other assets for retirement or family.

Ownership, beneficiary arrangements, insurable-interest rules, policy performance, taxation, and legal structure matter.

The point is not that everyone should use insurance for charity.

The point is that legacy planning should consider how different assets can be matched to different missions.

Giving With a Warm Hand

Legacy does not have to wait until death.

Perhaps you want to help a grandchild with education. Maybe you want to help a child buy a first home, support a family member starting a business, take the entire family on a trip, or see a ministry expand.

If the retirement plan shows that you have sufficient resources, some giving may be more meaningful while you are alive.

You get to see the impact.

You get to participate in the story.

You get to explain why the gift matters.

That does not mean giving away money you may later need. Your independence and your spouse's security come first.

But once the plan establishes what is reasonably safe, generosity can become part of retirement—not merely part of the estate.

Teach Before You Transfer

A person can spend forty years accumulating wealth and transfer it to someone in forty minutes.

That does not mean the recipient knows how to manage it.

If you expect to leave meaningful assets, part of your legacy may need to be education.

Talk about saving, investing, debt, taxes, work, generosity, responsibility, and the sacrifices that created the family's resources.

Explain what you hope the money makes possible.

Explain what you hope it does not become.

The greatest inheritance may not be the money itself.

It may be knowing how to steward it.

The Parable of the Talents and the Responsibility of the Receiver

In Matthew 25, Jesus tells the parable of servants entrusted with resources by their master. The passage has a broader spiritual meaning than financial investing, but stewardship is central to the story.

What is entrusted to us carries responsibility.

That principle applies not only to the person leaving wealth, but also to the person receiving it.

An inheritance is not merely a reward.

It is something newly entrusted.

Helping the next generation understand that may be one of the most valuable things we pass on.

Tell the Stories Behind the Money

Imagine inheriting your grandfather's watch.

It may have modest financial value.

But then you learn he wore it every day for thirty years while building the business that supported your family.

The value changes.

Money works the same way.

An investment account is just a number until the next generation understands why it exists, what sacrifices created it, what you believed, and what you hoped they would do with the opportunities it provides.

Tell those stories.

Write them down.

Record them.

Your estate plan transfers property.

Your stories transfer purpose.

Consider an Ethical Will

An ethical will is not a legal will and does not distribute property.

It is a personal document that can communicate values, faith, lessons, family stories, hopes, gratitude, advice, and love.

Imagine leaving your children or grandchildren a letter beginning:

"Here are the things life taught me that I hope you will remember."

That letter may someday mean more than the investment account.

For a faith-based retirement plan, an ethical will can also explain the beliefs that shaped your decisions, the Scriptures that mattered to you, the mistakes from which you learned, and the kind of life you hope future generations will pursue.

Passing on Faith Without Trying to Control From the Grave

There is a delicate balance in legacy planning.

We want to transmit values.

But we should be careful about using money as a tool to control adult children long after we are gone.

Trusts can be appropriate for many legitimate reasons: minors, special needs, creditor concerns, financial immaturity, blended families, business interests, or other circumstances.

But there is a difference between wise protection and attempting to script every decision future generations will make.

We can teach.

We can model.

We can encourage.

We can structure assets prudently.

But ultimately, the next generation must choose what it believes and how it will live.

Faith passed through example is usually stronger than faith enforced through conditions.

Family, Church, and Community Do Not Have to Compete

Some people feel tension between leaving money to family and giving to church or charity.

It does not always have to be either-or.

A well-designed plan may allocate different assets to different purposes.

Perhaps children receive assets that are efficient for them. Perhaps a charity receives an asset particularly suited to charitable transfer. Perhaps life insurance creates additional legacy capacity. Perhaps lifetime giving allows the family to participate in generosity together.

The objective is not to divide the estate according to a formula someone else says is biblical.

The objective is to prayerfully and thoughtfully decide what responsibilities and missions your resources should continue serving.

A Family Meeting Can Prevent Future Conflict

For some families, a family meeting can be extremely valuable.

You do not need to disclose every account balance.

But the people who will carry out the plan should understand what they need to know.

Who is the executor or personal representative? Who has power of attorney? Who is trustee? Where are documents located? Who are the financial, tax, legal, and insurance professionals? What is the long-term-care plan? Are there unusual estate provisions? What charitable intentions should be understood?

Clarity today can prevent resentment tomorrow.

Do Not Let Your Children Meet Your Advisors at Your Funeral

If you expect a financial professional, attorney, accountant, or other advisor to help your spouse or children after your death, introductions should happen before they are needed.

Your spouse should know who to call.

Adult children may benefit from knowing where important professional relationships exist.

The first conversation should not occur while everyone is grieving.

Relationships are easier to rely on when they already exist.

Mark and Lisa Define What They Want to Pass On

Originally, Mark and Lisa's estate plan was simple:

"Whatever is left goes to the children equally."

There is nothing inherently wrong with that.

But after working through their Purpose Driven Retirement plan, they begin asking better questions.

Priority one: protect the surviving spouse.

Priority two: preserve their own independence and ability to fund care.

Then they want to help grandchildren with education.

They want to continue supporting their church.

They want their children to inherit meaningful resources without making inheritance the purpose of their children's lives.

And they want to take the entire family on a major trip while they are still healthy enough to enjoy it.

Suddenly, legacy is not something that begins when Mark and Lisa die.

It is happening now.

The family trip creates memories.

Education funding creates opportunity.

Giving expresses faith and values.

Insurance may provide protection and leverage.

The estate plan directs what remains.

And conversations with the family transmit the meaning behind it all.

That is a living legacy.

Your Purpose Driven Legacy Exercise

Before talking about trusts, tax strategies, or legal documents, answer these questions.

1. Who matters most to us?

2. What do we want them protected from?

3. What do we want our money to accomplish after we are gone?

4. What would we rather do for people while we are still alive?

5. Which churches, ministries, charities, or causes matter deeply to us?

6. If we left money to our children tomorrow, are they prepared to manage it?

7. Are there family circumstances requiring special planning?

8. Who would handle our finances if we could not?

9. Who would make healthcare decisions?

10. Do our beneficiary designations match our intentions?

11. Does our family know where important documents are?

12. Have we made our financial life unnecessarily complicated?

13. What values do we want children and grandchildren to remember?

14. What stories do we want to preserve?

15. What role should generosity play during our lifetime?

16. What role should generosity play after our death?

17. Could a donor-advised fund, charitable trust, insurance strategy, or other planning tool improve the way we accomplish those goals?

18. Are we choosing a tool because it serves the mission—or creating a mission to justify the tool?

19. What does "enough" mean for our own retirement?

20. If money were removed from the equation entirely, what would we want our legacy to be?

That final question is the heart of the chapter.

What Will They Say About You?

Imagine your family gathering years from now.

Your grandchildren are telling stories.

What do you hope they say?

"He accumulated a lot of money."

Perhaps.

But maybe you would rather hear:

"He loved being with us."

"She was incredibly generous."

"They lived their faith."

"They helped people quietly."

"They took us places we never would have experienced."

"He taught me how to handle money."

"She taught me why giving mattered."

"They always made family a priority."

"They loved their church and their community."

"They enjoyed the life God gave them."

Those statements have very little to do with net worth.

And almost everything to do with purpose.

Estate Planning Is a Process

Estate planning is not something you finish once and place permanently in a drawer.

Children marry. Grandchildren arrive. Relationships change. Assets change. Tax laws change. You move. Someone dies. A business is sold. Beneficiaries mature. Charitable priorities evolve.

Review the plan periodically and after major life events.

The purpose may remain the same.

The tools may need to change.

From Legacy Back to Life

We have spent the last several chapters protecting the plan and considering what ultimately happens to what remains.

But now we need to turn our attention back to the life still in front of us.

You may have the income plan.

The investment strategy.

The tax plan.

The healthcare plan.

The long-term-care plan.

The insurance.

The estate documents.

But on Monday morning, when nobody expects you at work anymore, what are you going to do?

That is where retirement planning becomes retirement living.

And it is where the bucket list returns—not simply as a list of vacations, but as a combination of adventures, passions, family experiences, service, mission, and God's work.

Part VI — Living Your Purpose Driven Retirement (And Mission)

◆

A bucket list and a mission do not compete. Retirement can hold adventure, family, passions, rest, generosity, service, and God's work in the same life.

Chapter 13

What Are You Retiring To?

Your Bucket List, Your Mission, and the Life Still Ahead

Retirement Is Not the Finish Line

For decades, retirement planning has been presented as a finish line.

Work. Save. Invest. Retire.

But retirement is not the end of the story. It is the beginning of a different chapter.

The financial plan matters because it helps fund that chapter. The deeper question is what you intend to do with it.

Many people can tell you the exact date they want to retire. Far fewer can tell you what they are retiring to.

That distinction matters.

Bring Back the Bucket List

I do not want this faith-based edition to turn retirement into an endless list of obligations.

You are allowed to have fun.

You are allowed to travel.

You are allowed to buy the boat, learn the guitar, play more golf, see the national parks, sit on the beach, take the grandchildren to Disney, restore an old car, write a book, or spend a month in Italy.

A Purpose Driven Retirement should not eliminate the bucket list.

It should make the bucket list better.

The goal is to build a life that includes personal adventures, passions, family experiences, rest, generosity, service, and mission.

God's Work and a Great Vacation Can Exist on the Same List

Sometimes people of faith feel guilty about enjoyment.

If I have resources, should I really spend money traveling when I could give more away?

That is a worthwhile question, but guilt should not automatically provide the answer.

Ecclesiastes repeatedly recognizes the goodness of receiving and enjoying the fruits of our labor as a gift from God. Enjoyment and generosity do not have to be enemies.

You can take the family vacation and support the mission.

You can enjoy the lake house and serve your community.

You can play golf on Tuesday and mentor someone on Wednesday.

You can celebrate what you have been given without worshiping what you have been given.

Balance is the point.

A Better Bucket List Has More Than One Kind of Dream

Consider building your retirement bucket list in several categories.

Adventure: Where do you want to go? What do you want to see or experience?

Family: What memories do you want to create with the people you love?

Personal Growth: What do you want to learn, build, write, study, or master?

Relationships: Who deserves more of your time?

Health: What physical goals or experiences matter while you are able?

Generosity: What giving would bring you joy?

Service: Who could benefit from your experience, time, or attention?

Faith: How do you want your relationship with God to deepen?

Mission: What work might still be yours to do?

Now the bucket list becomes more than a collection of purchases. It becomes a picture of the life you want to live.

Retirement Changes the Currency From Money to Time

During your working years, money often feels scarce and time feels even scarcer.

In retirement, the relationship changes.

You may finally have more control over your time.

That makes time one of your most valuable retirement assets.

Psalm 90:12 asks God to teach us to number our days so that we may gain a heart of wisdom.

That verse is not meant to make us afraid of time. It reminds us that time is finite and therefore valuable.

Your retirement plan should budget money.

Your retirement life should budget time.

Do Not Save Every Dream for Later

Retirement is not one long, uniform season.

The early years may include greater health, mobility, energy, and willingness to travel.

Later years may be quieter.

That is not bad. It is simply different.

This is why the bucket list should have a time dimension.

Some dreams are physically demanding. Some require travel. Some involve grandchildren while they are still young. Some opportunities exist only for a season.

Do not assume that because the money will still be there at 80, the opportunity will be too.

The Go-Go, Slow-Go, and No-Go Idea

Retirement planners sometimes describe retirement in three broad phases: the go-go years, the slow-go years, and the no-go years.

The labels are imperfect, and every person ages differently, but the concept is useful.

In the earlier years, you may travel more, spend more, and pursue physically demanding experiences.

Later, life may become more local and less active.

Eventually, healthcare and assistance may consume more attention.

A good retirement plan should recognize that spending may not occur in a straight line.

And a good bucket list should recognize it too.

What Have You Been Postponing?

Think about the sentence you have probably said many times: “Someday, when I have more time...”

What comes next?

I'll travel. I'll volunteer. I'll spend more time with my grandchildren. I'll get involved at church. I'll learn to play piano. I'll fish more. I'll write. I'll reconnect with old friends. I'll get healthier. I'll study Scripture more seriously.

Retirement may be the someday you were talking about.

Do not arrive there and immediately invent another reason to postpone the life you said you wanted.

You Are Retiring From a Job, Not From Usefulness

One of the most damaging cultural ideas about retirement is that usefulness ends with employment.

It does not.

Your employer may no longer need your labor. That does not mean your family, church, community, or world no longer needs what you know.

Decades of experience do not disappear when you receive your last paycheck.

Leadership. Technical knowledge. Patience. Professional judgment. Relationships. Life lessons. Mistakes. Wisdom.

Those things may become more valuable because you finally have the time to share them.

Purpose Does Not Require a Pulpit

When we say "mission," some people immediately imagine becoming a missionary, teaching Sunday school, or working for a church.

Those may be wonderful callings.

But mission can look much more ordinary.

Mentor a young business owner. Coach a grandchild. Help a widow understand paperwork. Serve meals. Build houses. Volunteer at a hospital. Teach financial literacy. Use professional skills for a nonprofit. Drive someone to an appointment. Call a lonely friend. Help a neighbor.

Mission is not defined by whether the activity looks religious.

Colossians 3:23 encourages us to work wholeheartedly, as for the Lord. The principle can extend beyond paid employment: ordinary work can carry extraordinary purpose.

Jesus Washed Feet

In John 13, Jesus washed the feet of His disciples.

It is one of the most powerful images of leadership in Scripture because the person with the greatest authority took the position of a servant.

Retirement may give you an unusual opportunity to practice that kind of leadership.

You may no longer need the title. You may no longer need the corner office. You may no longer need anyone to know that you were the one who helped.

Perhaps retirement is a season when experience and humility can finally work together.

The question becomes less, "Who reports to me?" and more, "Whose feet can I wash?"

Not literally, necessarily.

But who can you serve?

From Achievement to Contribution

Working life often rewards achievement: promotion, income, recognition, production, status.

Retirement can invite a different scoreboard: contribution.

Who is better because you had time for them?

What organization is stronger because you helped?

What child or grandchild learned something because you taught it?

What problem became smaller because you showed up?

Achievement asks, "What did I accomplish?"

Contribution asks, "Who benefited?"

There is room for both. But retirement may be an especially good season to rebalance them.

The Grandparent Opportunity

For those who have grandchildren, retirement can create an extraordinary opportunity.

Grandchildren may remember the trips and gifts. But they may remember the conversations even more.

Teach them to fish. Take them to lunch individually. Tell them stories about their parents when they were young. Teach them how to save. Show them generosity. Bring them to volunteer. Let them see you pray. Ask what they are excited about. Attend the game, recital, graduation, or school event.

Legacy is often transmitted through ordinary time.

Mission Can Include Your Money

Not every person can physically serve in the same way.

Health, geography, caregiving, and other responsibilities may limit what you can do.

Financial resources can become part of the mission.

Support someone else doing work you believe in. Fund a scholarship. Help a church expand. Support a missionary. Help a family through a crisis. Create a charitable fund. Give anonymously.

Your retirement income plan tells you what you can spend.

Your stewardship plan helps you decide what some of that spending can accomplish.

But Do Not Turn Giving Into Another Competition

Even generosity can become a scoreboard.

Who gave more? Whose name is on the building? Who made the largest gift?

Jesus repeatedly challenged public displays of righteousness done for recognition.

Giving should not become another form of status.

Sometimes the most meaningful gift is the one almost nobody knows about.

The purpose is impact, not applause.

What If Your Mission Is Your Family?

Some people will read a chapter about mission and feel pressure to launch a nonprofit.

You do not need to.

Perhaps your mission in this season is caring for a spouse. Helping aging parents. Being present for grandchildren. Supporting an adult child through a difficult season. Rebuilding a relationship. Creating a stable home where family gathers.

Those things count.

Purpose is not measured by audience size.

What If You Still Want to Work?

Retirement does not require never earning another dollar.

You may want to consult, start a small business, teach, work part-time, serve on boards, turn a hobby into income, or return to a profession in a limited role.

The question is whether work now serves your life—or whether your life still serves the work.

Financial independence can change the relationship.

You may finally be able to say yes only to work that matters.

A Sabbath From Identity

Retirement can reveal how much identity was tied to occupation.

People ask, "What do you do?" and for forty years you had an immediate answer.

Then suddenly the answer changes.

That can be unsettling.

Your value was never your title. Your identity was never supposed to depend entirely on your business card.

A season of rest may help separate who you are from what you produced.

That can create space for a healthier question: "Who am I called to be now?"

The Distractions Do Not Retire When You Do

Retirement creates time, but time does not automatically create purpose.

Television can consume it. Social media can consume it. News can consume it. Politics can consume it. Golf can consume it. Shopping can consume it. Even volunteering can consume it if we say yes to everything.

The danger is not any one activity. The danger is allowing distraction to make the decisions for us.

If we do not intentionally decide what deserves our time, something else will decide for us.

A Fractured World Needs Grounded People

We live in a period when disagreement can quickly become contempt.

Neighbors become opponents. Political differences become moral judgments. Social media rewards outrage. Competition can replace community.

Even people with sincere faith can spend six days immersed in anger, comparison, fear, and division and then hope that one hour on Sunday will somehow reset everything.

That is not a political observation as much as a spiritual one.

Jesus' command to love our neighbor does not contain an exception for the neighbor who votes differently, irritates us, competes with us, or sees the world differently.

That does not mean every behavior is acceptable or every disagreement should disappear.

It means disagreement does not relieve us of the responsibility to love.

Love Thy Neighbor Is a Retirement Mission

What if one of the great missions of retirement is simply becoming a better neighbor?

You have more time.

Notice people. Learn names. Check on someone. Invite people over. Help with a project. Listen. Bring a meal. Offer a ride. Be the calm person in a divided room.

Retirement can create the margin required to live out values that working life sometimes crowded out.

Your Calendar Reveals Your Priorities

If I looked at your retirement calendar six months from now, what would it tell me matters?

Family? Health? Church? Travel? Friends? Service? Learning? Prayer? Rest?

Or would it show that retirement became a collection of appointments and distractions?

A financial plan allocates dollars.

A purposeful retirement also allocates days.

Put the Bucket List on the Financial Plan

Do not keep the bucket list in a separate notebook while the financial plan assumes generic spending.

Put actual dreams into the plan: Alaska cruise, family reunion, mission trip, RV purchase, kitchen renovation, grandchildren's education, annual charitable giving, national parks, second home—whatever matters.

Assign approximate costs and time frames.

Now the retirement plan can answer a much better question than, "Can I retire?"

It can begin answering, "Can I afford the retirement I actually want to live?"

Create a Mission Budget Too

If giving and service matter, they deserve space in the plan.

Perhaps you want a defined annual giving amount. Perhaps you want a separate mission or generosity fund. Perhaps you want to reserve money for spontaneous opportunities to help people. Perhaps volunteer work requires travel or expenses.

Budgeting for generosity does not make generosity less heartfelt.

It makes room for it.

The Permission to Spend

One of the surprising challenges of retirement is that disciplined savers can struggle to spend.

For forty years the rule was: save the money.

Then retirement arrives and the plan says: use the money.

That transition can be emotionally difficult.

A good retirement plan should create not only permission to retire, but permission to spend within reasonable boundaries.

If the plan demonstrates that the family vacation, charitable gift, or bucket-list trip is affordable, spending that money is not necessarily irresponsible.

The money was accumulated for a reason.

The Permission to Give

The same thing can happen with generosity.

People may want to give but worry that every dollar leaving the portfolio threatens retirement.

Planning can help establish guardrails.

How much is reasonably safe? What reserves must remain? What healthcare risks need protection? What does the surviving spouse need?

Once those responsibilities are addressed, the plan may create permission to give with greater confidence.

Generosity and prudence can coexist.

Mark and Lisa Build Two Bucket Lists

Mark and Lisa sit down with a blank sheet of paper.

At first they create the traditional list: Italy. National parks. Take the grandchildren to Disney. Rent a beach house for the entire family. Learn to play pickleball. Attend a major golf tournament.

Then they create another list: mentor younger couples at church, help fund a scholarship, volunteer together several times a year, spend individual time with each grandchild, support a ministry they care about, write down family stories, host more dinners at their home.

At first, these look like two different lists.

Then Lisa asks, "Why are these separate?"

They combine them.

Now the bucket list includes Italy and service. Golf and grandchildren. The beach house and generosity. Adventure and mission.

That is the point.

A Purpose Driven Retirement is not a choice between enjoying life and serving others.

It is designing a life where both belong.

Your Purpose Driven Bucket List

Take a blank sheet of paper and create your list.

Do not edit yourself at first.

Write down everything: places you want to go, things you want to learn, people you want to spend time with, family experiences, things you want to own, things you want to stop owning, physical challenges, creative goals, faith goals, giving goals, service goals, relationships you want to repair, people you want to mentor, stories you want to preserve, work you still want to do, and things you want to do simply because they sound fun.

Then mark each item with one of three letters:

N — Now: best pursued while health, time, or circumstances make it possible.

L — Later: meaningful, but reasonably postponable.

O — Ongoing: something you want woven throughout retirement.

Now add two more questions beside every major item: What will this require financially? Why does this matter to me?

Those answers turn a wish list into a retirement plan.

Your Mission Statement for Retirement

Now try to complete this sentence: "In this next chapter of life, I want to use my time, experience, relationships, and resources to..."

Do not worry about making it sound impressive.

Perhaps: "...love my family well, experience the world with my wife, help younger people avoid mistakes I made, and use what we have been given to help others."

Or: "...stay healthy enough to enjoy my grandchildren, deepen my faith, travel, and serve my church and community."

Or simply: "...be present."

Your mission statement can change.

The purpose is direction, not perfection.

Come Back to This Book

This book should not be a one-time read.

Life is distracting. Markets change. Tax laws change. Health changes. Family changes. Priorities drift.

And sometimes we drift.

We can begin with sincere intentions and gradually find ourselves spending more time reacting than living.

That is why I want you to return to these pages.

Once a year, perhaps around your birthday, anniversary, retirement date, or the beginning of a new year, revisit the questions.

What matters most now? What changed? What are we postponing? Where have we drifted? Are our money and time still pointed toward the things we say matter? How are we doing as spouses, parents, grandparents, friends, neighbors, stewards, and people of faith?

Do not use the review as a guilt exercise.

Use it as a compass.

The Annual Purpose Driven Review

Once each year, review five areas:

1. MONEY — Is the financial plan still healthy?
2. FAMILY — Who needs more of us right now?
3. HEALTH — What are we doing to preserve independence and ability?
4. BUCKET LIST — What should happen this year rather than someday?
5. MISSION — Where can our time, experience, faith, or resources make a difference?

Then choose a few priorities.

Not fifty.

A few.

Purpose becomes powerful when it reaches the calendar.

Retirement Is Not About Escaping Work

At its best, retirement is not an escape.

It is freedom.

Freedom from needing every hour to produce income. Freedom to choose where attention goes. Freedom to be more intentional with time. Freedom to enjoy. Freedom to serve. Freedom to give. Freedom to rest. Freedom to pursue work because it matters rather than because the mortgage requires it.

That freedom is why the financial plan exists.

The Life Still Ahead

You spent decades preparing for retirement.

Now retirement must be used.

Take the trip. Call your children. Play with the grandchildren. Rest. Learn. Give. Serve. Build something. Teach something. Forgive someone. Reconnect. Sit quietly. Pray. Go somewhere you have always wanted to go. Help someone who cannot repay you.

Do not confuse responsible planning with postponing life indefinitely.

James 4 reminds us that life is brief and that tomorrow is never entirely ours to command.

That is not a reason for recklessness.

It is a reason for intention.

You have a bucket list.

You may also have a mission.

You do not have to choose between them.

Live both.

Next: Chapter 14 — Staying Grounded: When Life, Money, and the World Pull You Off Course

The next chapter will build directly on the idea of returning to this book as a compass.

We will talk about distraction, comparison, fear, politics, markets, consumerism, social media, busyness, and the slow drift that can separate our daily lives from the values we say matter most.

And we will create a practical framework for getting grounded again—financially, relationally, and spiritually—when life inevitably pulls us off course.

Chapter 14

Staying Grounded

When Life, Money, and the World Pull You Off Course

Drift Rarely Happens All at Once

Most people do not wake up one morning and decide to abandon everything they say matters.

Drift is usually quieter than that.

One busy week becomes a busy month. One missed dinner becomes a pattern. One hour scrolling through the news becomes three. A disagreement becomes resentment. A financial concern becomes fear. A desire for security becomes an obsession with accumulation.

Eventually, our calendar, attention, money, and relationships can tell a very different story from the values we claim to hold.

That is why staying grounded requires intention.

Sunday Is Not Supposed to Carry the Other Six Days

For many people of faith, Sunday becomes a reset button.

We worship. We pray. We ask forgiveness. We remember what matters.

Then Monday arrives.

The phone starts ringing. Markets move. Work demands attention. Someone posts something infuriating. Traffic is terrible. A neighbor annoys us. The news tells us whom to fear. Social media tells us whom to envy. Advertising tells us what we still need.

By Saturday, we may be living very differently from the person we intended to be on Sunday.

The answer is not shame.

The answer is alignment.

Faith was never intended to occupy one hour of one day. The challenge is carrying what we say we believe into the ordinary decisions of the other six.

Retirement Does Not Automatically Fix This

People sometimes imagine retirement as the moment life finally becomes peaceful.

Maybe.

But removing a job does not remove distraction.

In fact, retirement can create more unstructured time for worry, comparison, outrage, spending, television, social media, or constant consumption of news.

Financial independence gives you greater control over your time.

It does not tell you what deserves that time.

That part still requires wisdom.

The Battle for Your Attention

Attention is one of the most valuable resources you possess.

Companies compete for it. Politicians compete for it. Media organizations compete for it. Social platforms compete for it. Advertisers compete for it.

Why?

Because attention influences behavior.

What you repeatedly look at affects what you think about. What you repeatedly think about affects what you fear, desire, resent, pursue, and eventually do.

Philippians 4:8 encourages believers to direct their thoughts toward what is true, honorable, just, pure, lovely, commendable, excellent, and worthy of praise.

That does not require ignoring problems.

It does require asking whether our information diet is forming us into the people we want to become.

Informed Is Different From Consumed

You should know what is happening in the world.

You should understand issues that affect your family, finances, community, and country.

But there is a difference between being informed and being consumed.

If checking the market ten times a day does not change the financial plan, what is it accomplishing?

If watching another three hours of political commentary does not change how you vote, serve, pray, give, or treat your neighbor, what is it accomplishing?

If the information leaves you chronically angry but no more useful, perhaps the problem is no longer information.

It is attention.

Fear Is a Terrible Financial Planner

Fear often disguises itself as prudence.

What if the market crashes?

What if taxes rise?

What if Social Security changes?

What if inflation returns?

What if I need long-term care?

What if I live to 100?

Those are legitimate planning questions.

But there is a difference between planning for risk and living in fear of risk.

Matthew 6 warns against allowing worry about tomorrow to consume today. That does not mean we should refuse to plan. Scripture contains plenty of examples of preparation and stewardship.

The distinction is important:

Planning says, "This could happen, so let us prepare wisely."

Fear says, "This could happen, so I cannot enjoy today."

Greed Can Disguise Itself as Security Too

There is another form of drift that financial planning must confront.

Enough keeps moving.

You thought $1 million would make you feel secure. Then you reached it and decided $2 million would.

Then $3 million.

At some point, the pursuit of security can become indistinguishable from the pursuit of more.

Luke 12:15 records Jesus warning that life does not consist in the abundance of possessions.

That does not condemn wealth.

It challenges the belief that more wealth can eventually solve the deeper problem of uncertainty.

No portfolio can eliminate uncertainty.

A good plan creates reasonable confidence.

It should not promise control over everything.

Comparison Is Expensive

Comparison can damage both contentment and financial plans.

Your neighbor buys a larger house.

Your friend takes a luxury cruise.

Someone posts pictures from Europe.

A former coworker joins an expensive club.

Suddenly, things you never wanted begin to feel necessary.

Comparison creates spending without purpose.

First Timothy 6 speaks about godliness with contentment as great gain.

Contentment does not mean refusing ambition or enjoyment.

It means your definition of enough does not have to be dictated by someone else's lifestyle.

Your Neighbor Is Not Your Competition

We live in a culture that often encourages us to rank ourselves.

Who earns more?

Who owns more?

Whose children are more successful?

Whose retirement looks better?

Who belongs to the right group?

Who has the right political views?

Who is winning?

But Jesus did not tell us to outperform our neighbor.

He told us to love our neighbor.

That is a very different way to live.

Love Your Neighbor Does Not Mean Agree With Your Neighbor

Mark 12 places loving our neighbor among the greatest commandments.

That does not mean pretending every idea is equally wise or every behavior is acceptable.

Love does not require intellectual surrender.

You can disagree strongly.

You can vote differently.

You can establish boundaries.

You can oppose an idea.

You can defend what you believe is true.

But another person's disagreement does not automatically make that person your enemy.

And even when someone behaves like an enemy, Jesus' teaching becomes more challenging rather than less: Matthew 5 calls believers to love enemies and pray for those who persecute them.

That is a demanding standard.

It is also radically different from the incentives of modern outrage culture.

The Goal Is Not Political Apathy

This book is not asking you to stop caring about government, public policy, elections, or the future of the country.

Citizenship carries responsibilities.

Vote.

Learn.

Participate.

Speak.

Serve.

Advocate for what you believe is right.

But politics should not become an idol.

No political party can carry the full weight of your identity, hope, morality, community, and purpose.

Government has legitimate functions. It is not God.

Political engagement can be part of responsible citizenship without becoming the organizing principle of your emotional life.

Render to Caesar—and Remember the Rest of the Sentence

In Matthew 22, Jesus is asked about paying taxes to Caesar.

His answer is famous: render to Caesar what belongs to Caesar, and to God what belongs to God.

We discussed this principle in the tax chapter because it provides a useful framework for civic and financial responsibility.

Paying legitimate taxes is part of participating in an organized society. Roads, courts, defense, public safety, infrastructure, and other public functions require resources.

At the same time, Jesus' answer draws a boundary.

Caesar does not get everything.

Government has a role. It is not the ultimate object of loyalty, identity, meaning, or worship.

That balance matters financially, politically, and spiritually.

Taxes: Stewardship Without Obsession

Tax planning is valuable.

Needlessly paying more tax than the law requires does not make someone more virtuous.

Use available deductions, credits, account structures, charitable strategies, Roth planning, estate strategies, and other legitimate tools when they improve the plan.

But tax avoidance should not become the mission of the retirement plan.

Sometimes paying tax is the consequence of having income, realizing gains, or using money for something worthwhile.

The objective is not zero tax at any cost.

The objective is thoughtful, lawful, and efficient stewardship.

Money Is a Tool, but Tools Can Become Masters

Money can provide security, opportunity, generosity, independence, experiences, healthcare, education, and enormous good.

But a tool becomes dangerous when it becomes the master.

Matthew 6:24 warns that we cannot serve both God and money.

Notice the wording.

The problem is not possessing money.

The problem is serving it.

A Purpose Driven Retirement asks money to serve the mission—not the other way around.

The Market Does Not Know Your Name

The stock market does not know you retired.

It does not know you are nervous.

It does not know you promised your grandchildren a vacation.

It does not care that the television commentator sounded confident.

Markets will rise and fall.

A retirement strategy should anticipate that reality.

One of the purposes of a written plan is to prevent every market movement from becoming an emotional referendum on your future.

If nothing material has changed in the plan, a frightening headline should not automatically create a financial decision.

Do Not Confuse Activity With Progress

Investors often feel better when they are doing something.

Sell.

Buy.

Move to cash.

Change funds.

Chase the winner.

Avoid the loser.

But activity and progress are not the same.

Sometimes the most disciplined financial action is no action.

The same is true in life.

A full calendar does not prove a meaningful life.

Busyness can become another distraction from purpose.

The Phone Can Steal Retirement One Minute at a Time

Imagine retiring with roughly 2,000 additional waking hours each year that once belonged to work.

That sounds like freedom.

Now imagine giving three hours a day to television, news, social media, and casual phone use.

That is more than 1,000 hours a year.

The point is not that screens are evil.

The point is that small habits can quietly consume enormous portions of the life you worked decades to gain.

Retirement needs boundaries around attention just as a portfolio needs boundaries around risk.

Create a Personal Rule of Life

A rule of life is simply a set of intentional rhythms that helps keep your daily life aligned with what matters.

It does not need to be complicated.

Perhaps your retirement rhythm includes prayer before checking the phone.

Exercise several mornings each week.

One day each week for grandchildren.

Church on Sunday.

A monthly date with your spouse.

One volunteer commitment.

Defined news windows rather than all-day television.

Quarterly financial reviews instead of daily portfolio checking.

Regular time outdoors.

Annual travel.

Intentional rest.

The schedule is not the purpose.

The schedule protects the purpose.

Rest Is Not Laziness

Some high-achieving people struggle with retirement because rest feels unproductive.

But Scripture establishes a rhythm of work and rest from its earliest pages.

Rest is not the absence of purpose.

Sometimes rest preserves our ability to pursue purpose.

Take the afternoon off.

Sit on the porch.

Read.

Nap.

Walk.

Pray.

Do something with no measurable return.

You do not have to optimize every hour of retirement.

Service Is Not Busyness Either

There is an opposite problem.

Some retirees replace a sixty-hour workweek with sixty hours of committees, boards, church responsibilities, volunteer assignments, and family obligations.

Service is good.

Exhaustion is not automatically holy.

Jesus served constantly, but the Gospels also describe Him withdrawing from crowds to pray.

You are allowed to say no.

Every good opportunity is not necessarily your assignment.

Forgiveness May Be One of the Best Uses of Retirement

Some people enter retirement carrying decades of unresolved hurt.

A sibling.

An adult child.

A former business partner.

A neighbor.

A church conflict.

An old friend.

Forgiveness does not mean pretending harm did not happen or returning to unsafe relationships.

But bitterness consumes attention.

Ephesians 4 calls believers away from bitterness and toward kindness, compassion, and forgiveness.

You worked too hard for your retirement to spend it replaying an argument from 1998.

Reconciliation Is a Legacy Too

Imagine leaving your children a large inheritance but also leaving them a family divided by unresolved conflict.

Now imagine leaving somewhat less money but helping restore relationships before you are gone.

Which legacy is richer?

Not every relationship can be repaired.

Reconciliation requires more than one willing person.

But where you can make a call, apologize, listen, forgive, or reopen a door, retirement may provide the time and perspective to try.

Faith Should Change the Way We Treat People

It is possible to know Scripture and still be cruel.

It is possible to attend church and still be dishonest.

It is possible to give generously and still treat employees, servers, family members, or strangers poorly.

Faith that never reaches behavior becomes easy to compartmentalize.

The retirement mission is not simply to attend more religious activities.

It is to become more aligned with the person our faith calls us to be.

More patient.

More generous.

More truthful.

More forgiving.

More willing to serve.

More difficult to provoke.

More interested in people than in winning.

Your Financial Plan Can Help You Live This Out

This may sound far removed from retirement planning.

It is not.

Money affects time.

Money affects stress.

Money affects choices.

A strong retirement plan can create margin.

Margin to spend time with family.

Margin to volunteer.

Margin to give.

Margin to leave a toxic job.

Margin to care for someone.

Margin to travel.

Margin to rest.

Financial independence is powerful because it can give you greater freedom to decide what deserves your life.

Mark and Lisa Notice the Drift

Six months after retirement, Mark and Lisa realize something surprising.

They are busier than expected.

Mark watches financial television every morning and checks the portfolio several times a day.

Lisa has agreed to so many volunteer commitments that she feels as scheduled as she did while working.

They are going to church.

They are financially secure.

They are checking things off the bucket list.

But something feels off.

So they return to their Purpose Driven Retirement plan.

They ask the questions again.

What matters most?

Where have we drifted?

What are we doing because it matters—and what are we doing simply because it filled the space?

Mark limits portfolio checking and turns off the television after a short morning update.

Lisa steps away from two committees and keeps the volunteer work she finds most meaningful.

They reserve Friday afternoons for each other.

They call the grandchildren more.

They begin inviting neighbors to dinner.

Nothing dramatic happened.

They simply recalibrated.

That is what a good plan should allow us to do.

The Purpose Driven Reset

When life feels scattered, return to five questions.

1. WHAT HAS MY ATTENTION?

What am I thinking about most? Is it useful, healthy, and aligned with what matters?

2. WHAT HAS MY TIME?

Does my calendar reflect my priorities?

3. WHAT HAS MY MONEY?

Does my spending, saving, investing, and giving reflect what I say I value?

4. WHO HAS MY HEART?

Am I investing enough in the people I love? Is there someone I need to forgive, call, help, or simply spend time with?

5. WHAT IS MY MISSION RIGHT NOW?

Not ten years ago. Not what someone else expects. What is mine to do in this season?

These five questions can bring a surprising amount of clarity.

When You Drift, Return—Do Not Quit

You will drift.

So will I.

That is part of being human.

The objective is not perfect alignment every day.

The objective is noticing when we are off course and returning.

A pilot can be slightly off course many times during a flight and still reach the destination because corrections are made along the way.

Retirement works similarly.

Financial plans require course corrections.

So do lives.

Use This Book as a Compass

Write in this book.

Underline things.

Disagree with me.

Change your answers.

Fold pages.

Return to the exercises.

Once a year, reread the chapters that matter most to your current season.

If markets are frightening you, return to the investment and income chapters.

If taxes are frustrating you, return to the tax chapter and remember that efficiency—not obsession—is the goal.

If family circumstances change, return to the care and estate chapters.

If you feel bored, return to the bucket list.

If you feel lost, return to purpose.

If you feel angry at the world, return to love thy neighbor.

This is not meant to be a book you finish once and forget.

It is meant to be a book you return to and use.

Grounded Does Not Mean Passive

Being grounded does not mean ignoring injustice, refusing ambition, avoiding difficult conversations, or pretending the world is fine.

It means acting from conviction rather than constant reaction.

It means knowing what you believe without needing to hate everyone who disagrees.

It means planning for risk without worshiping safety.

It means enjoying money without serving money.

It means participating in society without asking politics to become your religion.

It means serving others without losing yourself.

It means remembering that retirement is not merely the absence of employment.

It is stewardship of a finite amount of life.

A Final Grounding Exercise

Complete these sentences.

I am most easily distracted by...

When I am afraid financially, I tend to...

When I compare myself with others, I tend to...

The people who deserve more of my attention are...

The things I want less of in retirement are...

The things I want more of are...

I need stronger boundaries around...

I need to forgive...

I need to spend less time worrying about...

I need to spend more time doing...

My money is supposed to serve...

My retirement is supposed to make possible...

My faith should be visible in the way I...

The neighbor I need to do a better job loving is...

Right now, the most important thing God may be asking me to do is...

Keep your answers.

Come back to them.

The Quiet Measure of a Successful Retirement

At the end of retirement, nobody receives a trophy for having the lowest tax bill.

There is no award for checking a portfolio every morning.

No one wins because their account balance peaked at the highest number.

Financial outcomes matter because they support life.

But the quiet measures may matter more.

Did you love well?

Did you provide responsibly?

Did you enjoy what you were given?

Did you help anyone?

Did you grow?

Did you forgive?

Did you remain generous?

Did you make memories?

Did you use your time intentionally?

Did your faith become something you lived rather than merely something you said?

Those questions belong in a retirement plan too.

Next: Chapter 15 — Your Purpose Driven Retirement Plan: Bringing Money, Faith, Family, and Mission Together

The next chapter will begin pulling the entire book into one integrated framework.

We will bring together purpose, retirement income, investments, taxes, Social Security and pensions, healthcare, long-term care, insurance, estate planning, the bucket list, giving, family, and mission.

The goal will be practical: turn everything we have discussed into a written Purpose Driven Retirement Plan that a reader can actually use, review, and revisit.

Chapter 15

Your Purpose Driven Retirement Plan

Bringing Money, Faith, Family, and Mission Together

A Plan Is More Than a Stack of Recommendations

By this point, we have covered a lot.

Retirement income. Investments. Social Security and pensions. Taxes. Healthcare. Long-term care. Insurance. Estate planning. Giving. Family. The bucket list. Mission. Faith. Purpose.

That can feel overwhelming.

But the purpose of comprehensive planning is not to give you fifteen separate plans.

It is to create one coordinated plan for one life.

Your investment strategy should support your income strategy. Your income strategy should communicate with your tax strategy. Your tax strategy should consider Medicare. Your insurance should protect the risks that could disrupt the plan. Your estate plan should direct what remains. Your giving should fit the resources available. Your bucket list should be funded. And all of it should serve the people, values, and purposes that matter most.

Integration is where planning becomes powerful.

The Financial Plan Is the Architecture; Purpose Is the Reason for the Building

A retirement plan can be technically excellent and still fail the person it was designed for.

Imagine a plan that minimizes taxes, maximizes expected returns, preserves every possible dollar for heirs, and leaves the retiree afraid to spend money, travel, give, or enjoy life.

Was that successful?

Perhaps mathematically.

Not necessarily humanly.

Jesus asks in Mark 8 what it profits a person to gain the whole world and forfeit the soul. Retirement planning should never confuse financial optimization with the purpose of life.

The spreadsheet is important.

But the spreadsheet works for you.

Start With What Matters Most

Before reviewing accounts, begin with a blank page.

Write down the people who matter most.

Write down what you want retirement to feel like.

Write down the experiences you do not want to miss.

Write down the responsibilities you believe you have.

Write down what you want to give.

Write down who you want to help.

Write down what you believe God may still be calling you to do.

Those answers become the design criteria for the financial plan.

Step 1: Define Your Purpose

Complete these statements:

Retirement will be successful for us if...

The people we most want to protect are...

The experiences we most want to have are...

The relationships we most want to strengthen are...

The causes, church, ministries, or communities we want to support are...

The work or service we may still want to do is...

The legacy we want to leave is...

Our faith should influence our retirement by...

This is the foundation.

Step 2: Define What Enough Looks Like

Enough is not a universal number.

For one household, enough may mean a modest home, family nearby, church, and reliable income.

For another, it may include extensive travel, a second home, large charitable gifts, and substantial family support.

The question is not what your neighbor needs.

It is what your life requires.

Calculate the income needed for essential expenses, discretionary lifestyle, healthcare, travel, giving, family support, and reserves.

Then separate what is required from what is desired.

Both matter. They simply have different priorities.

Step 3: Build the Retirement Paycheck

Retirement income should be designed, not improvised.

Identify dependable income sources such as Social Security, pensions, annuity income where applicable, rental income, or other recurring resources.

Then determine the gap that investments must fill.

Consider when each income source begins, whether it changes with inflation, what happens at the death of a spouse, and how taxes affect the amount actually available to spend.

The goal is not merely gross income.

It is a sustainable after-tax retirement paycheck.

Step 4: Give Every Account a Job

Do not let accounts exist simply because they have always existed.

Ask what each asset is for.

Near-term spending?

Emergency reserves?

Growth?

Future healthcare?

Long-term care?

Legacy?

Charitable giving?

Tax flexibility?

Survivor protection?

Different accounts can perform different jobs.

When every dollar has a purpose, the portfolio becomes easier to understand and often easier to manage.

Step 5: Coordinate Investments With Spending

Investment risk should not be considered in isolation from the retirement paycheck.

If money will be needed soon, exposing all of it to substantial market volatility may create unnecessary sequence risk.

If money may not be needed for twenty years, keeping all of it in cash may create a different risk: inflation and lost purchasing power.

The investment plan should match time horizon, income needs, risk capacity, risk tolerance, tax characteristics, and purpose.

Do not chase returns simply because another investment performed better last year.

Your portfolio has a job.

Step 6: Build Tax Flexibility

Tax planning should look across years rather than treating each tax return as an isolated event.

Ask whether retirement creates lower-income years. Consider whether Roth conversions, capital-gain realization, charitable giving, withdrawal sequencing, qualified charitable distributions when eligible, or other strategies could improve the long-term outcome under applicable law.

But remember our earlier principle from Matthew 22.

Render to Caesar what is Caesar's—and to God what is God's.

Pay what is legitimately owed. Plan intelligently. Do not make minimizing tax the object of worship.

The objective is not zero tax at any cost.

The objective is thoughtful, lawful, and efficient stewardship.

Step 7: Coordinate Social Security and Pensions

Social Security and pension elections can affect the household for decades.

Do not evaluate a claiming decision only by asking which option produces the largest first-year check.

Consider longevity, survivor income, inflation adjustments, taxation, other assets, health, work plans, and the needs of both spouses.

For households with federal, state, municipal, military, or other specialized retirement systems, the interaction among pension elections, survivor benefits, healthcare, life insurance, and retirement accounts can be especially important.

These decisions should be integrated rather than made in separate silos.

Step 8: Protect Healthcare and Independence

Estimate healthcare costs.

Plan the bridge if retiring before Medicare eligibility.

Understand Medicare choices and how income can affect premiums under applicable rules.

Identify which resources would pay for unexpected medical costs.

Then address long-term care.

Where would you want care?

Who would provide it?

What can you self-fund?

What risk should potentially be transferred?

How will the healthy spouse remain secure?

Healthcare planning is not simply about paying bills.

It is about preserving choices.

Step 9: Protect the People You Love

Review life insurance and other risk-management tools through the lens established in Part V.

What happens financially if one spouse dies?

What income disappears?

What debts remain?

Could a pension change?

Is there a permanent legacy objective?

Would long-term-care or chronic-illness provisions improve the plan?

Could insurance create useful asset leverage?

Protection first. Leverage second. Product last.

Step 10: Build the Estate and Legacy Plan

Coordinate wills, trusts where appropriate, powers of attorney, healthcare directives, beneficiary designations, insurance, account ownership, charitable intentions, and family communication.

Do not stop at who gets what.

Ask what you want to pass on.

Faith.

Wisdom.

Opportunity.

Generosity.

Stories.

Responsibility.

An example.

Your estate transfers property.

Your legacy transfers meaning.

Step 11: Fund the Bucket List

Bring the actual retirement life into the financial plan.

List the trips.

The family experiences.

The hobbies.

The home projects.

The adventures.

The things you have postponed for years.

Estimate cost and timing.

Prioritize physically demanding experiences earlier when appropriate.

Do not wait until every uncertainty has disappeared.

That day will never arrive.

Prudence should create freedom, not permanent postponement.

Step 12: Build Giving Into the Plan

If generosity matters, give it a place in the plan.

Annual church giving.

Charitable gifts.

Family assistance.

A donor-advised fund.

Qualified charitable distributions when applicable.

Charitable trusts for appropriate circumstances.

Legacy gifts.

Life-insurance strategies where suitable.

Spontaneous generosity.

Do not begin with the tax deduction.

Begin with the impact.

Second Corinthians 9 teaches that giving should come from the heart rather than compulsion.

A plan can create the financial confidence to give joyfully rather than fearfully.

Step 13: Build a Mission Budget

Mission often requires resources.

A volunteer trip may cost money.

Mentoring may require time.

Helping grandchildren may require travel.

Serving at church may affect the weekly schedule.

Supporting a cause may require recurring gifts.

If mission matters, treat it as something real enough to budget for.

Your money plan and your calendar should both make room for it.

Step 14: Simplify

Complexity has a cost.

Too many accounts, policies, passwords, advisors, investment strategies, properties, and disconnected documents can make retirement harder to manage.

Complexity becomes especially dangerous if a spouse or child must take over during illness or incapacity.

Simplification does not mean eliminating every sophisticated strategy.

It means complexity should earn its place.

If a strategy cannot be explained clearly, understood by the people who depend on it, and maintained over time, ask whether it belongs.

Step 15: Put the Plan on One Page

After the detailed analysis is complete, create a one-page summary.

It should answer:

What matters most?

How much do we need to live?

Where does our retirement paycheck come from?

What are our major risks?

What are the next three financial actions?

What are the next three life priorities?

What are we giving?

What are we protecting?

What are we looking forward to?

What is our mission in this season?

The technical plan may be hundreds of pages.

The life plan should be understandable on one.

Your Purpose Driven Retirement One-Page Plan

PURPOSE — In this chapter of life, we want to use our time, relationships, experience, faith, and resources to...

PEOPLE — The people we most want to protect and spend time with are...

ENOUGH — Our target lifestyle requires approximately...

PAYCHECK — Our retirement income will come from...

INVESTMENTS — Our portfolio's primary jobs are...

TAXES — Our major tax-planning opportunities are...

HEALTH — Our healthcare and long-term-care plan is...

PROTECTION — The major risks we have transferred or intentionally retained are...

BUCKET LIST — The three experiences we most want to accomplish next are...

GIVING — Our giving priorities are...

LEGACY — What we most want to pass on is...

MISSION — Right now, we believe our time and resources can make the greatest difference by...

NEXT ACTIONS — The next three things we need to do are...

The Plan Needs Guardrails

A plan should create freedom, but freedom works better with boundaries.

How much cash reserve do we maintain?

How much portfolio decline can the plan reasonably tolerate?

How much can we give without threatening essential goals?

How much can we spend on major bucket-list items?

What circumstances would cause us to reduce spending?

What circumstances would allow us to spend or give more?

When do we review insurance?

When do we update estate documents?

Guardrails reduce the need to make every decision from scratch.

The Plan Needs a Decision Hierarchy

When difficult choices arise, use an order of priorities.

First: protect basic needs and dignity.

Second: protect the surviving spouse and dependent family.

Third: protect essential healthcare and care needs.

Fourth: maintain reasonable financial resilience.

Fifth: fund the life you actually want to live.

Sixth: help family responsibly.

Seventh: give and create broader impact.

Eighth: maximize what remains as legacy.

This order will not fit every family perfectly.

But it prevents a common mistake: sacrificing today's responsibilities merely to maximize tomorrow's inheritance.

When Goals Conflict

Real planning involves tradeoffs.

Should we give $50,000 to charity or help a child with a home?

Should we take the expensive family trip or convert more money to Roth?

Should we keep the house or move closer to grandchildren?

Should we buy long-term-care insurance or retain the risk?

Should we retire now or work two more years?

There may be no mathematically perfect answer.

Return to purpose.

Which decision best protects responsibilities while advancing what matters most?

Financial planning provides information.

Values make the final choice.

Faith Does Not Eliminate Uncertainty

A faith-based retirement plan should never imply that good planning guarantees good outcomes.

It does not.

Markets fall.

People become sick.

Spouses die earlier than expected.

Children struggle.

Tax laws change.

Plans break.

Faith is not a promise that uncertainty disappears.

Nor is planning evidence that we lack faith.

Proverbs repeatedly praises wisdom and prudent preparation.

We plan because we have responsibilities.

Then we acknowledge that not everything belongs to our control.

The Difference Between Control and Stewardship

Control says: I must guarantee the outcome.

Stewardship says: I will responsibly manage what has been entrusted to me.

Those are very different burdens.

You cannot guarantee your investment returns.

You can choose a reasonable strategy.

You cannot guarantee perfect health.

You can care for yourself and prepare for healthcare costs.

You cannot guarantee what your children will do with an inheritance.

You can teach, communicate, and structure the transfer wisely.

You cannot guarantee how long you will live.

You can use the days you have intentionally.

Stewardship gives us responsibility without pretending we are sovereign.

Mark and Lisa's Integrated Plan

Mark and Lisa now have something very different from the retirement plan they began with.

Originally, the question was: Can we retire?

Now their plan answers much more.

They know where their retirement paycheck comes from.

They understand which accounts fund near-term spending and which are intended for longer-term growth.

They have a tax strategy rather than simply filing tax returns.

They have coordinated Social Security and pension decisions.

They have healthcare and long-term-care plans.

They have reviewed survivor protection.

They have updated estate documents and beneficiaries.

They have identified what they want children, grandchildren, church, and charity to receive.

They have a bucket list with timing and estimated costs.

They have a giving plan.

They have a mission.

And they have agreed to return to the plan every year.

Their plan is no longer simply about not running out of money.

It is about using money well.

The Annual Purpose Driven Retirement Meeting

Once a year, sit down—alone, with your spouse, with family where appropriate, and with your professional advisors—and ask:

Are we still financially healthy?

Did our spending match what we expected?

Are income sources still working as intended?

Do investments still match their jobs?

Are there tax opportunities this year?

Did Social Security, pension, Medicare, or other rules change in ways that affect us?

Has health changed?

Has family changed?

Do insurance policies still fit?

Do estate documents and beneficiaries still reflect our wishes?

What did we accomplish from the bucket list?

What should move from Later to Now?

Did we give the way we intended?

Where did we serve?

Where did we drift?

What matters most in the year ahead?

Then update the plan.

Do Not Let the Review Become a Performance Evaluation

This annual meeting is not designed to tell you whether you were a good Christian, a good retiree, or a good person.

It is not a scorecard for guilt.

It is a recalibration.

Maybe you spent more than expected because the family had an incredible year together.

Maybe you gave less because healthcare costs rose.

Maybe a mission changed.

Maybe you traveled less because a grandchild needed you nearby.

Life happened.

The plan should respond to life—not punish you for living it.

When You Need Help

Some readers will enjoy building much of this themselves.

Others will reach this chapter and think:

"I understand the ideas. I just don't know how to put all of this together."

That is completely reasonable.

Retirement planning can involve investments, taxes, Social Security, pensions, Medicare, insurance, estate planning, charitable strategies, cash flow, and family decisions that interact with one another.

You do not have to become an expert in every subject.

A good advisor should help you understand the decisions, coordinate the moving parts, and translate complexity into a plan you can actually use.

The goal is not dependency on an advisor.

The goal is clarity and confident decision-making.

Advice Should Feel Like Guidance, Not Pressure

Financial planning involves important decisions and sometimes significant products or transactions.

You should understand why a recommendation is being made.

Ask:

What problem does this solve?

What are the costs?

What are the risks?

What are the alternatives?

What happens if we do nothing?

How does the advisor get paid?

What assumptions are being used?

What part is guaranteed and what part is not?

How does this affect the rest of the plan?

A recommendation should survive those questions.

If it cannot, slow down.

The Plan Is a Living Document

Your retirement plan is not finished when the binder is printed.

Retirement may last twenty, thirty, or forty years.

Everything will change.

Markets.

Tax law.

Family.

Health.

Goals.

Giving.

Technology.

Your understanding of purpose.

That is why the plan must live.

Return.

Review.

Recalculate.

Reprioritize.

Then keep living.

Your Purpose Driven Planning Checklist

☐ We have defined what a successful retirement means to us.

☐ We know approximately what our desired lifestyle costs.

☐ We understand where our retirement paycheck will come from.

☐ We have coordinated Social Security and pension decisions.

☐ Every major investment account has a job.

☐ We have a tax strategy, not merely a tax return.

☐ We have planned for healthcare.

☐ We have a long-term-care strategy.

☐ We have reviewed survivor protection and life insurance.

☐ Our estate documents are current.

☐ Our beneficiary designations match our intentions.

☐ Our family knows what it reasonably needs to know.

☐ We have identified our bucket-list priorities.

☐ We have a giving strategy.

☐ We have considered what "enough" means.

☐ We have identified the legacy we want to leave.

☐ We have written a retirement mission statement.

☐ We have a process for reviewing the plan annually.

☐ We know the next three actions.

Do not worry if every box is not checked today.

That is why you have a plan.

The Point of All This Planning

After fifteen chapters, it would be easy to conclude that retirement is enormously complicated.

In some ways, it is.

But complexity is not the point.

The point is freedom.

Freedom to wake up without wondering whether the money works.

Freedom to spend within the plan.

Freedom to give.

Freedom to help family.

Freedom to say no.

Freedom to say yes.

Freedom to travel.

Freedom to rest.

Freedom to serve.

Freedom to pursue the work God may still have for you.

The purpose of planning is not to spend retirement thinking about money.

It is to organize the money well enough that you can spend more of retirement thinking about everything else.

Next: Chapter 16 — The Retirement You Were Actually Planning For

The next chapter will bring the book toward its conclusion.

We will step away from accounts, strategies, and checklists and return to the question that started everything:

What is retirement for?

We will look at gratitude, enough, family, faith, service, enjoyment, legacy, and the courage to actually live the plan.

And we will begin preparing the reader for the final invitation: if putting all of these pieces together feels overwhelming, help is available—without pressure, obligation, or judgment.

Chapter 16

The Retirement You Were Actually Planning For

Enough. Gratitude. Courage. And the Life in Front of You.

You Were Never Really Saving for an Account Balance

For years, retirement may have been represented by a number.

$500,000.

$1 million.

$2 million.

A pension amount.

A Social Security estimate.

A retirement date circled on a calendar.

Those numbers mattered. They still matter.

But you were never really saving for an account balance.

You were saving for mornings.

For time.

For choices.

For family.

For travel.

For security.

For the ability to say yes.

For the ability to say no.

For the freedom to help someone.

For the freedom to rest.

For a life that no longer had to be organized primarily around earning the next paycheck.

The money was always supposed to fund something larger than itself.

The Question Changes

Before retirement, the question is often:

"Will I have enough?"

That is an important question.

But eventually, if the plan works, the question changes.

"What will I do with enough?"

That is where this entire book has been leading.

Enough is not the end of planning.

It is the beginning of freedom.

Enough Does Not Mean Excess

Enough is not a command to stop growing, earning, investing, or building.

It is not a universal dollar amount.

It is not a criticism of wealth.

Enough is the point at which money can begin to loosen its grip on your decisions.

You have reasonable provision for your needs.

You have prepared for uncertainty.

You have protected the people who depend on you.

You have resources for healthcare.

You have a plan for the future.

And now you can begin asking what the rest is for.

First Timothy 6:17-19 offers a useful perspective: those with resources are warned not to place their hope in wealth, but to enjoy what God provides and to be rich in good works and generosity.

Enjoyment and generosity appear in the same picture.

That balance is at the heart of Purpose Driven Retirement.

Gratitude Changes the Experience of Wealth

Two people can have the same financial resources and experience them completely differently.

One sees what is missing.

The other sees what has been provided.

One constantly compares.

The other is grateful.

One is afraid to spend.

The other spends thoughtfully.

One hoards because enough never arrives.

The other recognizes that resources can be used.

Gratitude does not eliminate ambition.

It changes the relationship with abundance.

James 1:17 reminds us that every good and perfect gift is from above.

That perspective can turn retirement from an entitlement into something received with gratitude.

You Do Not Have to Apologize for Enjoying Retirement

If you worked, saved, sacrificed, planned, and lived responsibly, you do not need to feel guilty every time you enjoy the fruits of that work.

Take the trip.

Order dessert.

Buy the tickets.

Spend the week at the beach.

Play golf.

Go fishing.

Renovate the kitchen if it will genuinely improve your life.

Enjoy dinner with friends.

Ecclesiastes recognizes enjoyment of work and its fruits as a gift.

The warning is not against enjoyment.

The warning is against allowing enjoyment, possessions, or wealth to become the source of identity and meaning.

You can enjoy the gift without worshiping the gift.

And You Do Not Have to Spend Just Because You Can

The opposite is also true.

Purposeful retirement is not a command to consume.

Maybe you do not want the bigger house.

Maybe you are tired of maintaining things.

Maybe another luxury purchase does not interest you.

Maybe the greatest improvement in your retirement would be owning less.

Financial independence gives you permission to stop performing wealth for other people.

You can choose simplicity because you prefer it.

Contentment is a form of freedom.

Retirement Is a Season, Not a Permanent Vacation

A vacation is wonderful partly because it is temporary.

Retirement may last decades.

If the entire plan is built around entertainment, eventually even entertainment can feel empty.

That is why the bucket list matters—and why the mission matters too.

Adventure gives life excitement.

Relationships give it connection.

Service gives it contribution.

Faith gives it grounding.

Rest gives it renewal.

Purpose helps these things belong together.

The First Year May Feel Strange

Retirement can be emotionally disorienting.

Even people who desperately wanted to retire can miss the structure, identity, relationships, and sense of usefulness that work provided.

You may wake up and think:

"Now what?"

That does not mean retirement was a mistake.

It means a major life structure disappeared.

Give yourself permission to learn the new rhythm.

You do not need to solve the next thirty years during the first thirty days.

Do Not Recreate the Job You Just Left

Some retirees immediately fill every empty hour.

Committees.

Projects.

Consulting.

Volunteer work.

Errands.

Obligations.

Before long, retirement has become another full-time job with worse boundaries.

Be careful.

Purpose does not require permanent busyness.

Leave margin.

Some of the best parts of retirement may happen in the spaces you did not schedule.

Your Spouse May Have a Different Retirement

Retirement is often planned financially as a household but experienced personally by two different people.

One spouse may want to travel constantly.

The other may want to stay home.

One wants golf.

The other wants grandchildren.

One wants to move.

The other never wants to leave the neighborhood.

One retires first while the other continues working.

These differences do not mean the plan failed.

They mean retirement requires conversation.

A shared life does not require identical interests.

Build a retirement with room for togetherness and individuality.

Family Is Not a Line Item

Financial plans often contain categories such as gifts to children, education funding, or inheritance.

But family is not simply a financial obligation.

Time may be the greater gift.

Call.

Visit.

Show up.

Listen.

Take the trip together.

Tell the stories.

Ask the questions.

Be available.

Deuteronomy 6 describes faith and instruction being woven into ordinary life—when sitting at home, walking along the road, lying down, and getting up.

Legacy often happens in ordinary moments, not formal speeches.

You May Be Needed More Than You Realize

Retirement can create something that younger generations often lack: margin.

You may have time to pick up a grandchild.

Help an adult child through a difficult week.

Sit with a friend at the hospital.

Mentor someone beginning a career.

Help a neighbor.

Serve at church.

Listen to someone who needs an hour rather than five minutes.

That availability has value.

Your usefulness did not expire with your employee badge.

The Greatest Return May Not Appear on a Statement

Financial professionals spend a great deal of time measuring returns.

Investment return.

Income return.

Tax savings.

Portfolio growth.

Those things matter.

But retirement contains returns that cannot be measured in basis points.

A grandchild who remembers every Tuesday afternoon with you.

A marriage that becomes stronger because you finally have time together.

A younger person whose life changes because you mentored them.

A church or charity strengthened because you served.

A family tradition that survives another generation.

A reconciliation that happens before it is too late.

Not every return belongs on a statement.

Generosity Changes the Meaning of Abundance

There is a difference between having resources and knowing what to do with them.

Generosity gives abundance direction.

Sometimes generosity is money.

Sometimes it is time.

Sometimes it is knowledge.

Sometimes it is forgiveness.

Sometimes it is hospitality.

Sometimes it is simply noticing someone.

Acts 20:35 preserves Jesus' teaching that it is more blessed to give than to receive.

That principle is not merely about charitable deductions.

It is about the kind of person abundance allows us to become.

Giving Does Not Require Ignoring Your Responsibilities

Generosity should not become financial recklessness.

Your spouse still needs security.

You still need housing.

Healthcare still matters.

Long-term care may still happen.

Family responsibilities remain.

Biblical stewardship includes provision as well as generosity.

That is why this book has spent so much time building the financial foundation.

Planning creates guardrails within which generosity can become more confident.

Sometimes the Best Gift Is Permission

Parents often want to help adult children but worry about creating dependency.

That is a legitimate concern.

Help can be structured thoughtfully.

Perhaps the gift funds education rather than lifestyle.

Perhaps it helps with a first home while the child contributes too.

Perhaps you match savings.

Perhaps you help during a genuine crisis.

Perhaps you give experiences rather than cash.

The purpose is not to control adult children.

It is to use resources in ways that create opportunity without removing responsibility.

Let Your Children See You Enjoy the Money Too

There is another lesson worth passing on.

Some children watch their parents save relentlessly for forty years and then refuse to spend a dollar in retirement.

What lesson does that teach?

Perhaps that money should always be feared.

Let them see responsible enjoyment.

Let them see that saving had a purpose.

Let them see you take the trip.

Let them see you give.

Let them see you help someone.

Let them see you say, "We planned for this."

That is financial education too.

Do the Things That Require You to Be Here

Some estate goals can be accomplished after death.

Many of life's best goals cannot.

Your estate can fund a grandchild's education after you are gone.

It cannot sit in the audience at graduation.

Life insurance can leave money to your children.

It cannot take them to dinner.

A charitable bequest can support your church.

It cannot let you participate in the work.

Do not reserve every act of generosity and love for the estate plan.

Some things require your presence.

There Is Courage in Spending

For lifelong savers, retirement spending can require courage.

The account balance may go down.

That can feel wrong.

But if the plan was designed to turn accumulated assets into retirement income, a declining balance may sometimes be evidence that the money is doing its job.

The objective is not careless depletion.

It is intentional use.

A retirement account is not a museum exhibit.

It is a resource.

There Is Courage in Giving

Giving can also require courage.

What if I need the money later?

That is why we plan.

Establish reserves.

Protect healthcare.

Model longevity.

Protect the spouse.

Stress-test the plan.

Then, where capacity exists, generosity can move from vague intention to action.

Do not let uncertainty automatically veto every meaningful gift.

There Is Courage in Saying No

Retirement freedom also means saying no.

No to obligations you do not need.

No to purchases designed to impress.

No to constant news.

No to relationships built entirely around conflict.

No to financial products you do not understand.

No to family expectations that would endanger your own security.

No to every invitation simply because your calendar is open.

A purposeful yes often requires several purposeful noes.

There Is Courage in Changing the Plan

You may discover that the retirement you imagined at 55 is not the retirement you want at 68.

Change it.

Maybe the RV was a dream until you rented one.

Maybe the second home feels like work.

Maybe travel matters less and grandchildren matter more.

Maybe you want to work again.

Maybe a ministry becomes important.

Maybe you move.

Maybe health changes everything.

The plan exists to serve your life.

Your life does not exist to remain loyal to an old plan.

Faith Is Not a Retirement Strategy

This distinction matters.

Faith is not another asset class.

Prayer is not a substitute for diversification.

Giving is not a guaranteed method for becoming wealthier.

Scripture is not a promise that believers will avoid illness, market losses, family difficulty, or financial uncertainty.

A faith-based retirement plan should never manipulate belief into a sales strategy.

Faith provides the foundation for how we understand stewardship, responsibility, generosity, contentment, service, hope, and purpose.

The technical planning still has to stand on its own merits.

And Financial Planning Is Not Salvation

A comprehensive plan can reduce uncertainty.

It can organize decisions.

It can identify risks.

It can create confidence.

It cannot guarantee tomorrow.

It cannot prevent death.

It cannot fix every relationship.

It cannot create meaning by itself.

That is an important boundary.

Money is useful.

Planning is useful.

Neither deserves the burden of becoming the source of ultimate security.

The Peace of Having a Plan

There is still something powerful about knowing the pieces have been considered.

The income works.

The investments have jobs.

The tax strategy is intentional.

Healthcare has been addressed.

Long-term care has been discussed.

The spouse is protected.

The estate documents are organized.

The children know what they need to know.

The bucket list is real.

The giving is intentional.

The mission has words.

You cannot control the future.

But you do not have to enter it unprepared.

Mark and Lisa Stop Planning for a Moment

Mark and Lisa have spent months working through their retirement.

They have run projections.

Reviewed Social Security.

Evaluated pensions.

Repositioned investments.

Discussed taxes.

Reviewed insurance.

Planned for healthcare and long-term care.

Updated estate documents.

Created a giving plan.

Built a bucket list.

Written a mission statement.

Then one evening Lisa asks a question.

"Are we done planning yet?"

Mark laughs.

Technically, no.

There will always be another review.

Another tax year.

Another market cycle.

Another decision.

But they realize something.

They have enough information to begin living.

So they book Italy.

They schedule the family beach week.

They increase their church giving within the plan.

Mark agrees to mentor a younger professional.

Lisa begins volunteering with an organization she cares about.

They reserve Friday afternoons for each other.

And they stop checking whether retirement is working every day.

They start living it.

The Plan Has Done Its Job When You Need It Less

This may sound strange coming from someone who believes deeply in planning.

But the goal of a retirement plan is not to make you think about retirement planning constantly.

The plan should eventually become infrastructure.

Like electricity in the walls.

You know it is there.

You maintain it.

You update it.

But you do not spend every evening staring at the wiring.

The best plan creates enough clarity that you can turn your attention back to life.

What If You Made a Mistake?

You will.

You may claim a benefit and later wish you had chosen differently.

An investment may disappoint.

You may spend too much one year.

You may miss a tax opportunity.

You may buy something you regret.

You may postpone something too long.

You may say yes when you should have said no.

Retirement does not require perfect decisions.

A strong plan can absorb many imperfect ones.

Learn.

Adjust.

Continue.

Grace Belongs in the Plan Too

A faith-based retirement book should leave room for grace.

Grace when you did not save enough early.

Grace when you made a financial mistake.

Grace when family relationships are complicated.

Grace when your retirement does not look like someone else's.

Grace when your faith feels stronger in one season and weaker in another.

Grace when the plan changes.

Grace does not eliminate responsibility.

It allows responsibility without requiring perfection.

What Do You Want the Next Ten Years to Say?

Forget the rest of retirement for a moment.

Think about the next ten years.

If health is reasonably good and the financial plan gives you choices, what would make those ten years meaningful?

Where would you go?

Who would you spend time with?

What would you learn?

What would you give?

Who would you help?

What would you stop doing?

What would you begin?

What relationship deserves attention?

What part of your faith do you want to deepen?

What would you regret leaving undone?

Write the answers down.

Ten years can disappear surprisingly quickly.

And If You Only Had Five?

This is not meant to be morbid.

It is meant to sharpen priorities.

If you knew you had five healthy years rather than twenty, what would move up the list?

Would you still postpone the family trip?

Would you still work three more years?

Would you call the person?

Would you give the gift?

Would you spend every morning watching the market?

Would you continue the argument?

Would you keep saying someday?

Psalm 90's invitation to number our days is not an invitation to fear death.

It is an invitation to value life.

Retirement Is a Gift of Margin

Not everyone gets a long retirement.

Not everyone gets financial independence.

Not everyone gets good health.

If you have been given some combination of time, health, resources, relationships, experience, and freedom, receive it with gratitude.

Then use it.

Not frantically.

Not selfishly.

Not guiltily.

Intentionally.

The Retirement You Were Actually Planning For

The retirement you were actually planning for was never simply the day you stopped working.

It was the morning you could wake up and decide what deserved your day.

It was having enough confidence to enjoy the money.

It was having enough wisdom not to worship the money.

It was being able to care for your spouse.

It was being present for family.

It was seeing places you dreamed about.

It was serving without needing recognition.

It was giving without fear.

It was resting without guilt.

It was passing something meaningful to the next generation.

It was remaining grounded when the world became noisy.

It was living your faith beyond Sunday.

It was having both a bucket list and a mission.

That is Purpose Driven Retirement.

One More Question

At the beginning of retirement planning, people ask:

"Do I have enough money to retire?"

After everything we have discussed, I hope you will also ask:

"Do I have a plan for what I am going to do with the life retirement gives me?"

Both questions matter.

The first helps you retire.

The second helps make retirement worth reaching.

Next: Conclusion — Go Live the Plan

In the conclusion, we will bring the reader back to the simplest message in the book: plan wisely, hold the plan with humility, remain grounded in faith, love people well, enjoy what you have been given, give where you can make a difference, and go live.

We will also make room for the reader who reaches the final page and says, "I need help putting this together."

The invitation will be simple: no pressure, no obligation, no judgment—just a conversation and help taking the next step.

CONCLUSION

Go Live the Plan

Plan Wisely. Hold It Humbly. Live It Fully.

You Have Done Enough Planning to Begin

We have covered a lot of ground together.

We have talked about retirement income, investments, Social Security, pensions, taxes, healthcare, long-term care, insurance, estate planning, family, giving, the bucket list, faith, service, legacy, and mission.

Those subjects matter because retirement is not one financial decision.

It is a life transition.

But there comes a point when more analysis stops improving the plan and begins delaying the life the plan was built to support.

You do not need perfect certainty before you begin.

You need enough clarity to move forward wisely.

The Goal Was Never Perfection

No retirement plan will predict every market return.

No tax strategy will anticipate every future law.

No healthcare projection will know exactly what care you will need.

No estate plan can control every family circumstance.

No bucket list will unfold exactly as written.

And no person of faith will live every day in perfect alignment with what he or she believes.

That is not failure.

That is life.

The purpose of the plan is not perfection.

It is direction.

Plan Wisely

Scripture does not ask us to ignore the future.

Proverbs repeatedly commends wisdom, diligence, counsel, and prudent preparation.

Planning is one way we care for the people who depend on us.

Build the income plan.

Manage investment risk.

Plan for taxes.

Understand healthcare.

Prepare for long-term care.

Protect the surviving spouse.

Organize the estate.

Review beneficiaries.

Create reserves.

Know what enough means.

Planning is not fear when it is done wisely.

It is stewardship.

Hold the Plan Humbly

James 4 reminds us that we do not control tomorrow.

That is not an argument against planning.

It is an argument against confusing planning with control.

Do the work.

Make the best decisions you can with the information available.

Then remain willing to adjust.

Markets will surprise you.

Life will surprise you.

God may surprise you.

A plan should provide direction without becoming an idol.

Enjoy What You Have Been Given

Retirement should contain joy.

Not someday.

Now.

Take the trip that fits the plan.

Have dinner with friends.

Play with the grandchildren.

Sit by the water.

Learn something.

Buy something you have wanted when it is reasonable.

Rest.

Ecclesiastes reminds us that enjoying the fruits of our labor is itself a gift.

Responsible enjoyment is not the enemy of stewardship.

It can be part of stewardship.

Give Some of It Away

Do not wait until death to become generous.

If the plan supports it, help while you can see the impact.

Give to the church.

Support the ministry.

Help the family.

Fund the scholarship.

Help the neighbor.

Create the charitable strategy.

Give your money.

Give your time.

Give your experience.

Give your attention.

Give your forgiveness.

Generosity is one of the ways resources become purpose.

Love People More Than the Plan

Plans exist for people.

Never reverse that order.

If your child needs you, be there.

If your spouse needs more time with you, listen.

If a friend is struggling, call.

If a relationship can be repaired, consider taking the first step.

Jesus' command to love our neighbor is not a retirement-planning technique.

It is a way of life.

Your financial independence can create something enormously valuable: the margin to practice it.

Keep the Bucket List

Do not throw away the bucket list because this is a faith-based book.

Keep adding to it.

Travel.

Adventure.

Family.

Food.

Sports.

Hobbies.

Learning.

Experiences.

Dreams.

Then add mission.

Service.

Giving.

Mentoring.

Faith.

Relationships.

Legacy.

The bucket list and the mission list were never supposed to compete.

They are both part of the life you are still here to live.

Ask What Is Enough

From time to time, return to the question:

"What is enough?"

Enough income.

Enough savings.

Enough security.

Enough house.

Enough stuff.

Enough work.

Enough news.

Enough worry.

Enough accumulation.

The answer will change over time.

But asking the question can keep more from automatically becoming the goal.

Come Back When You Drift

You will drift.

Your spending may drift.

Your portfolio may drift.

Your priorities may drift.

Your calendar may drift.

Your attention may drift.

Your faith may drift.

Return.

Open this book again.

Revisit the exercises.

Ask what matters now.

Ask where the money is going.

Ask where the time is going.

Ask who needs you.

Ask what you are afraid of.

Ask what you are postponing.

Ask what God may be calling you toward in this season.

Then make the next correction.

You do not need to start over.

You simply need to get pointed in the right direction again.

Your Retirement Mission May Change

Mission is not necessarily one grand assignment that lasts forever.

At 62, your mission may include travel, mentoring, and helping grandchildren.

At 72, it may include caregiving, church leadership, and philanthropy.

At 82, it may be encouraging family, sharing wisdom, praying for others, and receiving help with grace.

Purpose can change shape without disappearing.

As long as there is life, there can still be purpose.

Do Not Underestimate Ordinary Faithfulness

Not every meaningful retirement will produce a foundation, a book, a ministry, or a building with your name on it.

Perhaps your greatest contribution will be quieter.

A marriage loved well.

Children supported without being controlled.

Grandchildren who know your stories.

A neighbor who could count on you.

A church that was stronger because you showed up.

A young person who made a better decision because you listened.

A family that remembers generosity.

An example of faith that was visible on Tuesday as well as Sunday.

Ordinary faithfulness can become an extraordinary legacy.

One Day the Numbers Will No Longer Matter

There will come a day when nobody in your family cares what the S&P 500 did during your retirement.

They will not remember your marginal tax bracket.

They probably will not know whether your portfolio earned 6.8% or 7.4%.

They may not remember which Medicare plan you chose.

But they may remember the family trip.

They may remember that you came to every game.

They may remember the way you treated people.

They may remember that you helped when someone was struggling.

They may remember your faith.

They may remember your generosity.

They may remember what you taught them about money.

They may remember that you seemed grateful.

Those memories are part of the return on your retirement.

The Final Purpose Driven Retirement Questions

Before you close this book, answer these questions one more time:

Who matters most?

What is enough?

What needs to be protected?

What do I still want to experience?

What do I need to stop postponing?

Who can I help?

What can I give?

What do I want my family to remember?

Where have I drifted?

What am I afraid of that planning can reasonably address?

What am I afraid of that planning cannot control?

What is mine to do now?

And perhaps the simplest question:

Am I living the life I said all this planning was for?

Go Live It

You have worked.

You have saved.

You have sacrificed.

You have planned.

Now use the plan.

Protect what needs protecting.

Pay what you owe.

Invest wisely.

Spend thoughtfully.

Give generously.

Love your family.

Love your neighbor.

Serve where you can.

Rest when you need to.

Stay grounded.

Keep learning.

Keep adjusting.

Keep the bucket list.

Keep the mission.

Keep the faith.

And go live the life in front of you.

That is the purpose of Purpose Driven Retirement (And Mission).

YOU DO NOT HAVE TO FIGURE IT OUT ALONE

A Final Invitation

If you have reached this page thinking, "I understand the ideas, but putting all of these pieces together feels overwhelming," that is a reasonable response.

Retirement planning can involve investments, taxes, Social Security, pensions, Medicare, insurance, estate planning, charitable strategies, cash flow, family decisions, and the life you actually want to live. Those decisions interact.

Purpose Driven Retirement Planners offers readers the opportunity to meet with us for a no-cost, no-obligation conversation. There is no requirement to become a client and no expectation that you arrive with everything organized.

Bring your questions. Bring the plan you already have. Or simply bring the question: "Are we on the right track?"

Our goal is simple: help you understand where you are, identify what may deserve attention, and determine a sensible next step.

No cost. No obligation. Just help.

Scan to schedule a conversation

Calendly: www.calendly.com/pdrp

Purpose Driven Retirement Planners

Transformational guidance helping people's retirement dreams become reality.

OTHER BOOKS FROM PURPOSE DRIVEN PRESS

Continue the journey with these companion retirement-planning books:

Purpose Driven Retirement — How to Turn the Life You've Worked For Into the Life You've Been Planning For

The core retirement-planning guide: purpose, income, investments, taxes, healthcare, protection, legacy, and taking action.

Purpose Driven Federal Retirement — How to Turn Your Federal Employee Benefits Into the Life You've Been Planning For

A focused guide for federal employees navigating FERS, TSP, FEHB, FEGLI, Social Security, survivor decisions, taxes, and the transition into retirement.

A Purpose Driven Teacher Retirement — How to Turn Your Virginia School Benefits Into the Life You've Been Planning For (A Virginia Edition)

A Virginia-focused guide for public-school employees covering VRS, 403(b) and 457(b) plans, Social Security, healthcare, taxes, and retirement purpose.

Uncle Sam & Auntie IRMAA — How to Keep the Government from Becoming Your Biggest Expense in Retirement

An approachable guide to retirement taxes, Medicare, IRMAA, RMDs, Roth conversions, and planning ahead for the government's share.

Each book is designed to stand on its own while also working as part of a broader Purpose Driven retirement-planning library.

REFERENCES & RESOURCES

A Note on Sources

This book is written for a general audience rather than as an academic treatise, so references are intentionally selective. The sources below are primary or authoritative resources for rules and concepts that can change over time.

Financial, tax, Social Security, Medicare, estate, charitable, and insurance rules should be verified at the time a strategy is implemented. Scripture references throughout the book are intended to direct the reader to the cited passage in context; unless a translation is specifically named, narrative wording should be understood as summary or paraphrase rather than a quotation from a particular Bible translation.

Primary Financial and Government Sources

Internal Revenue Service (IRS): Retirement Plans and IRA Required Minimum Distributions; Publication 590-B, Distributions from Individual Retirement Arrangements; Publication 590-A, Contributions to Individual Retirement Arrangements; Qualified Charitable Distribution guidance; Roth account and conversion guidance; Publication 525, Taxable and Nontaxable Income; estate and gift tax guidance; donor-advised fund guidance. *www.irs.gov*

Social Security Administration (SSA): Retirement, spouse, survivor, divorced-spouse, earnings-test, and claiming guidance; benefit-estimate and retirement-planning resources. *www.ssa.gov*

Centers for Medicare & Medicaid Services (CMS) / Medicare: Medicare Parts A and B, enrollment, premiums, IRMAA, coverage, skilled nursing, home health, and long-term-care coverage information. *www.medicare.gov* | *www.cms.gov*

U.S. Securities and Exchange Commission (SEC) / Investor.gov: Investor education on diversification, risk, fees, investment products, fraud awareness, and working with investment professionals. *www.investor.gov*

FINRA: Investor education concerning brokerage accounts, investment products, risk, fees, and BrokerCheck. *www.finra.org*

Selected Scripture References Used Throughout the Book

Genesis 2:2–3 — work, completion, and rest

Psalm 24:1 — stewardship and ownership

Psalm 90:12 — numbering our days wisely

Proverbs 15:22 — counsel and planning

Proverbs 21:5 — diligence and planning

Proverbs 22:3 — prudence and preparation

Ecclesiastes 3 — seasons of life

Ecclesiastes 5:18–20 — enjoying the fruits of labor

Matthew 5:44 — loving enemies and praying for those who oppose us

Matthew 6:19–34 — treasure, money, and worry

Matthew 22:15–22 — rendering to Caesar and to God

Matthew 25:14–30 — stewardship and the parable of the talents

Mark 8:36 — wealth and the soul

Mark 12:28–31 — loving God and neighbor

Luke 12:13–21 — abundance, possessions, and the rich fool

John 13:1–17 — servant leadership and washing the disciples' feet

Acts 20:35 — the blessing of giving

2 Corinthians 9:6–8 — willing and cheerful generosity

Philippians 2:3–4 — considering the interests of others

Philippians 4:8 — directing attention toward what is worthy

Colossians 3:23 — wholehearted work and service

1 Timothy 5:8 — responsibility to provide for family

1 Timothy 6:6–19 — contentment, wealth, generosity, and hope

James 1:17 — gratitude for good gifts

James 4:13–17 — humility about tomorrow

Ephesians 4:31–32 — bitterness, kindness, and forgiveness

About the Author

Stuart Hunsicker is the Founder of Purpose Driven Retirement Planners. His work focuses on helping individuals and families coordinate the many moving parts of retirement into a plan built around what matters most.

His professional background includes retirement planning, Social Security, federal employee benefits, investment advisory work, tax-aware planning, insurance, estate and legacy coordination, and the broader life decisions that shape retirement.

His professional credentials include Chartered Financial Consultant (ChFC), Retirement Income Certified Professional (RICP), Tax Planning Certified Professional (TPCP), Certified Financial Fiduciary (CFF), Certified Christian Financial Counselor (CERTCFC), National Social Security Advisor (NSSA), Chartered Federal Employee Benefits Consultant (ChFEBC), and Federal Retirement Consultant (FRC), along with additional professional education and experience. The CERTCFC is especially relevant to this edition and to Stuart's approach of bringing biblical principles of stewardship, generosity, family responsibility, and purpose into the retirement-planning conversation.

Purpose Driven Retirement (And Mission) reflects a belief that financial planning is ultimately about more than money: it is about stewardship, family, independence, generosity, service, faith, and using the next chapter of life with intention.

www.ingramcontent.com/pod-product-compliance
Lightning Source LLC
LaVergne TN
LVHW100136061126
851857LV00010B/113
9798997745202